May Day, May We

by Claire Taft Sherman

DORRANCE
PUBLISHING CO
EST. 1920
PITTSBURGH, PENNSYLVANIA 15222

Dorrance Publishing Co
701 Smithfield Street
Pittsburgh, PA 15222
Visit our website at *www.dorrancebookstore.com*

ISBN: 978-1-4809-1033-1
eISBN: 978-1-4809-1355-4

CONTENTS

INTRODUCTION

This book is not for the faint-hearted nor the functionally illiterate. Parental discretion and a sense of humor is advised.

The statements in this book are divided into three parts. Part of the information is regarded as true by the experts in the field. Part of the information will be regarded as true eventually. Part of the information is false. The nonconforming ideas arose from the processes of inductive and deductive reasoning.

The suggestions are to be taken seriously, or not, as you prefer. The songs are to be sung. The tests are to be taken.

Most of the book was written in the late 1990s. I was unemployed again. The phrase "publish or perish" took on a whole new meaning for me. I wrote the research paper first but I couldn't find a magazine that would accept it, so I decided to write a book instead. I had stopped thinking in terms of a tome leaning toward the scholarly side and started working on a book that would sell like, *gasp*, *choke*, fast food.

If you read my book, I'll read yours.

-The Author

AMENDMENTS (PROPOSED)

The Constitution of the United States is hereby amended as follows:

1. No person shall be sentenced to death by the United States, or by any state, except for the crime of treason in time of war.
[Intent: to reduce the homicide rate.]

2. The human embryo shall not be considered a person under this Constitution.
[Intent: to avoid the necessity for the U.S. Supreme Court to rule on a philosophical question.]

3. Equality of rights under the law shall not be denied or abridged by the United States or by any state on account of gender.
[Intent: to make official the notion that men are not inferior to the other gender.]

4. The use, possession, transportation, manufacture, and sale of moderate amounts of alcohol, or of any product containing the same, shall not be prohibited by the United States. The use, possession, transportation, manufacture, and sale of moderate amounts of tobacco, or of any product containing the same, shall not be prohibited by the United States. The use, possession, transportation, manufacture, and sale of moderate amounts of marijuana, or of any product containing the same, shall not be prohibited by the United States.
[Intent: to reduce dependence on the unholy trio of alcohol, tobacco, and coffee.]

5. The House of Representatives and the Senate are hereby restrained and restricted from voting on bills which cover, include, and encompass separate and unrelated points, subjects, or topics.
[Intent: to advance the cause of law and order.]

6. The Senate of the United States shall be composed of one senator from each state, elected by the people thereof, for six years; and each senator shall have one vote.
[Intent: to reduce the number of elected government officials.]

7. The number of members of the House of Representatives shall be fixed at four hundred and ninety-nine.
[Intent: to provide employment opportunities for displaced U.S. Senators.]

8. The names of electors for President of the United States shall be presented to the person or persons who appoint or elect them independently of the names of electors for Vice-President of the United States. If an elector for President is pledged to vote for a particular candidate for President, and said presidential candidate belongs to an organized political party, the elector is required to make available to all interested parties the name of that party's preferred candidate for Speaker of the House in the next Congress,
[Intent: to remind the Vice-President of his duty to preside over the Senate and to remind the Speaker of the House of his duty to talk for the people in the majority.]

9. The President of the United States is hereby authorized to refuse to spend and disburse any appropriated funds in any fiscal year, at his discretion, if the Auditor General of the United States, or such other person as the President shall appoint, with the advice and consent of the Senate, declares that the amount of monies appropriated by the Congress for said fiscal year exceeds the anticipated income and revenues to the United States for the same fiscal year.
[Intent: to inspire the Congress to pass balanced national budgets.]

10. All broadcast facilities and cable networks disseminating information, of whatever kind or nature, to the public and the people should be considered common carriers and must give equal access at equitable rates to all parties interested in communicating with the public and the people via such media, provided the nature of such communications are not prohibited by law.
[Intent: to bring First Amendment rights of the people to television land.]

I wish. And don't remark "Be careful what you wish for, you might get it." The chances that all ten of the above amendments will be adopted in my lifetime, unaccompanied by other amendments which would negate their effects, are remote to non-existent. But I am a person who likes to take the long view. And in my long view, these amendments will be accepted some day.

BIRTH CONTROL

Human infants require a lot of care to thrive. Toddlers require a lot of oversight to survive. And children who have newly learned to run on two legs require a huge playground and an attendant in motion. That being true, it is reasonable to conclude that young fertile couples have frequent opportunities to conceive so that they may wait until their prior young one (or ones, in the case of twins,) has reached the age of perhaps four years, or has died, before trying to get another, without sacrificing rare chances to reproduce. Now breathe.

We welcome children born at optimum intervals in opportune seasons. All others are more apt to be accepted, rejected, neglected, or abused. (Yes, a parent can bond with an unwanted child, as a lover can bond with a sex partner he should never have had, but such bondage is chafing.) Human couples can try for spring, summer, fall, or winter births, whatever will work best for them. And people can avoid childbirth during the lean years, in years of disease, and in years of war and still have descendants, if we wish. And if we haven't messed up the whole shooting match. Why wouldn't we wish?

Those who believe women are obliged to deliver as many children as is humanly possible likely believe that parents and children are put on this earth to suffer, that life is a term of punishment. And further, there are some among us who believe God created human sexual passion without providing for "after the sex act" birth control. Can you imagine?

All women are, in a sense, the daughters of the moon. What we need for birth control, and all we need for birth control, in healthy adult females, is glimpses of that nearest celestial body and a natural compound with the properties of aspirin. The phases of the moon mark the passage of a post-adolescent, pre-menopausal person's monthly cycle. If her menstrual period is late, that is a good, although not a perfect, indicator that she has within her an idea for a baby, a genetic blueprint for a child. With all of eight weeks after conception before a human embryo becomes a fetus, most mature women with regular periods have time, provided they heed their early warning system, to halt the gestational process by inducing menstruation.

About this natural compound to consume: it doesn't have to be a "pill" developed by the modern medical profession; it could be an herb from the good old days. Queen Anne of England didn't have any children, did she? The essential specifications are that these agents be safe (when used as directed), effective (when used as directed), and inexpensive to obtain or produce (birth control being a necessity rather than a luxury). Get with it! If a women is sure she doesn't want to bring a child into the world several months down the line, she doesn't even have to take a pregnancy test. She just has to take "the Terminator."

Call inducing menstruation after conception abortion if you must, but distinguish it from surgical abortion. Surgical abortions are not birth control but the last clear chance to prevent disasters.

By the way, the female of the species' capacity for multiple orgasms is compensation for the pains experienced during labor. "Mother" nature wouldn't do a woman wrong, although male persons might. We must be fair. Women can also wrong men by converting them into fathers without their consent. Yes, yes, a trivial pursuit when stacked beside rape, robbery, and miscellaneous mayhem by the guys but a bump in the road of cordial relations all the same.

CALENDAR

Thirty days has September,
April, June, July, November,
January and February.
Wasn't that a lot of fun?
All the rest have thirty-one.
One more thing to remember:
Give Leap Year's day to February!

DEATH

Why do people die? Human beings die because, being mammals, they have the luck to bear young via the bisexual technique. Egg plus sperm induces gestation, which induces birth, which induces life, which induces death. The laws of biochemistry are binding. The alternative is copying by cloning or no reproduction at all. It is fun to run; it is heavenly to die; and it is damning to go slamming. Human girls expire when they give birth and become women and human males do not become men until their fathers die. Adam and Eve were evicted from the Garden of Eden for having incestuous sex with each other. [Eve was bone of Adam's bone.] They succumbed to temptation.

What's that? You as an individual would gladly live without sex, if only you could live forever? Won't work. If the human species is to continue to live into infinity, we must always see the ever-changing "present" environment through clear, untutored eyes. The eyes of young children.

But please, let me assure you no one need worry about the agonizing pain of burning after death. The concept of Hell as a place of fire and brimstone was developed by sexually frustrated people living in a hot climate. If Hell exists after death, it is absolute-zero cold and as dark as a black hole.

Our survival depends on foods derived from plants and animals. The proper disposal of our corpses would make them available to provide food for other living things in their turn. Let's vote. How many of you would be comfortable if earth's carnivores acquired a taste for human flesh? Then, plant food it is. Did I forget anything?

The dinosaurs. Well, people, at times, death is a matter for joking, but the final extinction of a species never is. Tyrannosaurus rex, and its cousins, were vast, fast, voracious meat eaters and unable or unwilling to practice birth control. As a result, as their numbers over expanded, the T. rexes ate all the members of the other dinosaur species that hadn't grown wings. When those were all gone, they ate any other animals they could catch. (Our tiny mammalian ancestors were very nimble.) Then the T. rexes ate each other. The last T. rex left on earth starved to death, the glutton. And the same thing could happen to us if we don't eat our vegetables.

ELEMENTARY EDUCATION

Little ape see, little ape do. Children are born imitators. The primary stage for human behavior is explaining the rules of conduct in a language all can understand. Our babies not being born fluent in English, or any other verbal language, we, their parents and teachers, predominately explain by example.

The instinctive way for all primates to learn is by observing others and copying their motions. *Homo sapiens* is not only the naked ape but also the vocal ape, and with our parrot tongues we even learn to speak our native language by listening to words and phrases spoken around us and repeating them. Over and over. The "Do what I say, not what I do" treatment isn't very effective with auditors of any age. With youngsters, who see their parents as heroic providers, it's impossible.

The concept of negation, as in "Do not run into the street," is one of the most difficult parts of speech to learn. Too often, a toddler's brain interprets that type of phrase as "Do run into the street" and then the little guy gets yelled at for, from his point of view, following orders. Sometimes, in the U.S. of A., these older babies are even punished when, in a burst of enthusiasm to show Mama and Daddy they have finally grasped the nettle of opposition, they start enunciating "No, no, no!" At every opportunity.

Rules for beings with immature brains must be very consistent and simply logical. When we wish a kid to understand that hitting others is wrong, and not to be done, hitting that inexperienced person, in the (usually worthy) attempt to teach him that disobedient actions have consequences results in confusion, as does hitting someone else in his presence. I comprehend, so do run on sentences.

That is to say, confusion results unless we hit a child to make him or her stop hitting another person, possibly a younger or smaller one. Then, sending two logically incompatible messages: "Hitting a person is permissible because I do it," along with "You're being punished because hitting a person is impermissible," generates cognitive collapse. If a child's mind were a personal computer, that type of correction would cause a crash. How often do you tell your kid, "Don't talk with your month full," with food in your own mouth? Never, right?

After a mental meltdown due to the simultaneous hit/don't hit admonition, the best we can hope for is the lesson learned: it's okay to hit a child once you become an adult, but not yet. And we may not get the best. We may get a bully who sincerely flatters a role model by hitting those smaller and weaker than himself. Or something worse. I will leave you and your imagination to envision the worst.

I have three words for parents who need to restrain a violent tyke who is injuring someone or something. Full body hug. I have four words for teachers who need to retrain boys who want to test their physical strength against each other. Wrestling matches with rules.

Moving along to what should be taught in kindergarten class that wasn't in that simple little book whose title I can never remember. The "Does a tree in the forest make a noise if it falls and nobody hears?" Buddhist cliché question. That depends on whether noise means a sound made or a sound heard. If the questioner is unwilling to define his terms, don't try to answer her question. As for the "What is the sound of one hand clapping?" banality, it is absurd on its denotative face. One hand can't clap. Why bother to utter the query or respond except as a juvenile game? There is a third type of trick inquiry, at least in the Western world. "How many angels can dance on the head of a pin?" That question assumes a fact not in evidence: that angels can dance, or cannot dance, on the head of a pin. All verbal child stuff. Play fair or go sit in a corner by yourself.

FREE SPEECH

While contests in life are inevitable, unregulated conflicts are avoidable. That is to say, they are avoidable provided we allow our opposition open avenues of expression. Face facts, friends: Free speech free-for-alls frustrate fatal fights. Forbidding fair falsehoods forces failures to fierce infractions. Say or slay! Debate or die! Rock or disco! Put down your guns and use your tongues.

How do non-lethal alternatives work out?

Most of us, now and then, have been kept awake when we wanted to sleep by the clash of ideas in our own heads. A sounder exchange of concepts occurs when two persons of unlike minds thrust with this notion and parry with that thought until interested and initially neutral observers can perceive a semblance of the truth and declare the battle ended. If the competitors have been evenly heard, if the referees are fair, if the sky is tranquil, the decisions of the judges will be accepted as final, even by any "losers"—at least, until the losers have had time to rest, recover from their insults, and prepare to verbally duel again. No rose-tinted lenses for me. Roses are for noses.

Ideally, we counter points of logic with tips of sense. Imperfectly, one person's wisdom is another person's emotional outburst. Conclusively and constitutionally, we protect almost all vocalization. In pursuit of truth, we free speech.

"I think, I feel, etc." position statements are therefore A-OK. An example is, "In my opinion, people who shout 'Fire!' in a crowded theater should be shot themselves." Contrarily, declarations of the type, "Let's track down the sons of guns wherever they are and line them up. Do it!" are unauthorized utterances. We do not and should not liberate attempts to persuade, cajole, entice, exhort, command, or demand actions which have irreversible and destructive consequences.

Our inward thoughts and feelings are our own. Our outgoing hurtful and deadly deeds can and should be checked. The exception is, the fleet may eat meat (of other species). The exception confirms the rule.

GENERAL WELFARE

Hey! Could I have your attention, please? We really, really need a welfare system in these United States. I'll tell you why, and I won't lie. Because most of us don't have a family farm to return to anymore—a family farm to earn a subsistence living on when paying jobs are scarce. All right, all right. I confess. My uncle still has a few acres left. Does yours?

At the same time, when one apparently gets something for nothing, it has a bad effect on one's character. What to do? What to do?

So let's end welfare as we now know it—the "as we now know it" being A.F.D.C. It is not by chance that this program was designed to pay the most money to people with dependent personalities, i.e., exhausted women who have however many children came along. (Some people will try anything to stop women's liberation.) Let's make welfare payments to people with assertive personalities as well. Let's make welfare payments to people without regard to the type of personality they have, or their gender, provided they are legitimately high school graduates and further provided that they do twenty hours of "volunteer" work a week which benefits the community (or a subset of it). I must be joking.

Throw out all of the bureaucratic rules! Oops! I take that back. Throw out most of the bureaucratic rules. People participating must file "What I will be doing and the hours I will be at work each week" papers with the Department of Ingenuity and Creativity. In general, people are more enthusiastic volunteers when they have written their own job descriptions. Nobody assigns anybody to a certain type of work except themselves. We will need some guidelines as to what constitutes community benefit, some investigator-auditors to make sure something resembling twenty hours of work is being done, and a hotline for taxpayers to report the fraud of not actually working. But we won't need any eligibility rules. Not even for income limits. Have your eyes deceived you? No. You may collect General Welfare payments even if you are a millionaire, provided you put in the twenty hours per (and are a high school graduate). Would you give up a tax loophole for it? I guess that depends on the comparative worth of the tax loophole versus the welfare payment.

This restrained proposal is based on only twenty hours of work so that people will have ample time to look for higher paying work, continue their formal education, and care for their children and spouses. Can you find anything wrong with that? You can? You must be smarter than I am.

What about parents in poverty with several minor children? I'm glad you asked me that question. To be sure, we provide additional limited assistance to them. Food checks, perhaps. Keeping up appearances before the neighbors and prospective employers is so important if one wants to return to the world of regular work. But the greatest part of that assistance should be in the form of waiving the zoning laws and codes of any kind or nature so that several people could legally live in a one-room dwelling. Yes, yes, yes to access to clean, safe water and a sanitary toilet; yes, yes to sound and fire-resistant construction, windows and roof included, and heat in freezing weather; and yes to an attractive exterior and a place to cook food. Maybe to a place to bathe, and maybe to a place to plug in the TV. No to unminimal rents for such quarters. Or, here's a novel idea: Two, or more, nuclear families sharing the same multi-room apartment or house. Or, RV parks are a possibility.

Theoretically, given a family with some income, lowering living expenses is an acceptable response to poverty. Practically, those poor children will be guaranteed a job when they grow up. Assuming the state in which they live has an adequate public school system and an adequate public health system, they will be fit to work. Both safe assumptions, right? What else will be needed for this to work but an ad campaign? "Stay in school, kids, so when you're grown, you won't hit the skids. You'll be able to buy, buy, buy that pie in the sky your ancestors couldn't reach." Yuck! Where's a poet when you need one?

Don't worry about the survival of established American businesses under this glorious approach. Be happy! They will still be competitive because they have superior means of raising c-c-capital.

What's wrong with compelling the poor to take minimum wage jobs that no one capable of adding and subtracting dollars and cents wants? Are those paltry paying positions within walking distance of low-cost residences? Chuckle! Do those subservient salary tasks allow parents to bring and supervise their playing children at the work site? Snicker! Are you going to force me to make a sarcastic remark about slave wages? Snort!

What's in General Welfare for the middle class taxpayer besides elimination of aid to families with dependent children? No more food stamps for individuals, no more unemployment compensation, no more rent subsidies for the poor, no more swollen government disability programs, no more guaranteed student loans, no more endowments for the arts, no more you name it, and no more Social Security benefits. Double oops! That last item is politically inconceivable, or so I've read many times. How about General Welfare plus revision of the existing Social Security system to pay a monthly bonus based on the approximate total number of hours a person has worked during his or her lifetime. The very old, like the very young, should not have to concern themselves overmuch with financial burdens. Let's not be preposterous about the formula and record keeping required to determine the bonus. Lastly, all General Welfare payments and Social Security payments to be subject to the income tax. Yup! Everybody gets and everybody pays.

And now for the really big question. The bottom line. How much is General Welfare going to cost? The simple answer is: more than I think it will and less than you think it will. The complicated answer is: try it and find out. If the U.S. Gross National Product goes up and the amount of money in circulation remains the same, it would seem to follow that we will be getting more value for our money. Oh, I can stretch a dollar....

Oh, shirk! I forgot the amount! Let's assume the Federal Statutory Minimum Wage times twenty for each week's payment.

HYMN[1]

O for a thousand tongues to sing
My dearest leader's praise,
The glories of my Sage and King,
The triumphs of his grace!

My precious shepherd and my Lord,
Assist me to proclaim,
To spread through all the earth abroad
The honors of thy name.

Jesus! the name that charms our fears,
That bids our sorrows cease,
'Tis music in the sinners' ears,
'Tis life, and health, and peace.

He speaks, and listening to his voice,
New life the dead receive;
The mournful, broken hearts rejoice;
The wretched poor believe.

Hear him, you deaf; your speaking tongue,
You mute, in his cause employ;
You blind, behold your savior come;
And leap, you lame, for joy.

---

[1]Slightly revised version of "O For a Thousand Tongues to Sing," Charles Wesley

IRELAND

Being an American, I must ask forgiveness from the Irish people and the British people for using their "troubles" as an example of what compromising can do for sticky situation. Having received it, I continue.

Step 1:   The monarch of Great Britain and Northern Ireland resigns the office of the titular head of the Church of England for herself/himself and her or his successors forever.

Step 2:   The British Parliament amends the Acts of Succession to the British throne as follows: heirs to the throne who are married to, or, if single, who have agreed to marry, a person of the Roman Catholic faith raised in the Republic of Ireland take precedence over any of the other heirs when the present sovereign dies.

Step 3:   Voters in England, Scotland, and Wales elect delegates to a convention to draw a written constitution to direct and command their government and laws. Said constitution will make provisions for a democratic government whose symbolic and titular head is a hereditary monarch and otherwise retain the best parts of their unwritten constitution.

Step 4:   The delegates referred to above draft a constitution for the United States of Britain and Ireland (with a different national name). As many factions as can be found in Northern Ireland are consulted as to the best interests of the people of the six counties.

Step 5:   The written constitution referred to above is presented to the inhabitants of England, Scotland, and Wales for their acceptance or rejection. The first principle of receptive contracts being, what the large print gives, the fine print takes away, the voters read all the articles carefully before casting their ballots.

If the constitution is accepted, the plan moves to step 6. If the constitution is rejected, the plan loops back to step 3. If at first you don't succeed, try again.

Step 6: The Republic of Ireland is invited to join this new union. If the idea is accepted in principle by an Irish government elected after the invitation was extended, the written constitution is suitably amended to be acceptable to both governments. If the idea is rejected in principle by the Irish government of the time, the plan waits until a new Irish government is elected which favors it.

Step 7: The new union and constitution referred to above are presented to the inhabitants of the Republic of Ireland for their acceptance or rejection. The Irish voters having recently elected a government which favors the idea, the union/constitution is, of course, reluctantly accepted.

Step 8: The appropriate authority of the United States of Britain and Ireland, successor to the United Kingdom, formally cedes authority over the six counties of Northern Ireland and the people thereof to the state of "Southern" Ireland, thereby automatically incorporating Northern Ireland into the United States of Britain and Ireland.

Step 9: The Archbishop of Rome excommunicates as many members of the Roman Catholic Church involved in this transformation as is possible.

Step 10: The appropriate authority amends the Acts of Succession to the throne so that there are very few restrictions on who the heirs may marry. They all live happily ever after.

If every man, woman, and child in the British Isles, save one, who hears of this compromise plan hates it, that does not necessarily mean it's a "good" settlement. But is it better than any alternative yet proposed? I await the verdict of history.

JESUS SPOKE

He came, he saw, he spoke. Possibly, Jesus spoke in Aramaic. He spoke, positively, in parables. These parables presented paradoxes, perhaps. At least, they presented paradoxes to people ruled by fear, resentment, and faithlessness.

Pardon my ponderous paraphrasing and read on. If we risk our lives to save others, our own lives will be literally spared. But if we try to preserve our lives, we will die. If we give liberally to the poor, we will be materially enriched many times over. But if we hoard our wealth, we will lose everything. If we apply moral laws only to ourselves, we will live in the heavenly kingdom. But if we judge others, we will be left out. If we love our enemies, we will win the war. But if we hate them, we will be defeated. Promises, promises, promises. Provided we supply seed-size belief and purposeful activity.

With relief I return to the graceful cadences of the King James Version of the Christian Bible for some practical advice. "But I say unto you, That ye resist not evil: but whosoever shall smite thee on thy right cheek, turn to him the other also. And if any man will sue thee at the law, and take away thy coat, Let him have thy cloke also. And whosoever shall compel thee to go a mile, go with him twain." Matthew 5:39-41. In other words, align with that control freak.

Fighting back would not be alignment. Surrendering one's life, or the whole of one's physical possessions, or one's liberty would not be redirection, the next necessary step. Making a measured, and unexpected, response to unjust demands by voluntarily doubling the help we are being compelled to provide would be both. The psychological neutralization of evil.

Gerald W. Piaget wrote *Control Freaks: Who They Are and How to Stop Them from Running Your Life*. He recommends, in the face of intimidation and manipulation, what he calls "the Aikido alternative" and I call Christian ethics. You may call it whatever you please, so long as you understand the concept.

You'll be sorry if you don't find your copy of the self-help book that best fits your needs and peruse the passages on the most appropriate responses to wrong doing. Very sorry. Go look for one immediately. I'll wait. While I'm waiting, I re-read *The Taming of the Shrew* by W. Shakespeare.

One closing paradox: The more we praise Jesus of Nazareth, the less important he becomes.

P.S. The paradoxical Jesus may not have understood the "leveling the playing field" concept. When the enemies of a righteous man are saying, It is better that one man should die than that a whole nation should perish; said righteous man does not have much alternative but to reply, Hey, it is better that a whole nation should perish than that one man should die.

P.S.S. I know of an Old Testament wise man who made a major blunder. Some women are so ethnic-centered they would rather see their babies die than be raised by a mother who is not their blood kin. For future reference, your majesty, when two women claim the same child as their own, send for an experienced midwife. Let her observe the reactions of the baby to the two women who claim it as their child, and accept the midwife's decision. I am tempted to throw up my hands and say, "Lord, what fools some men be." However, my female brain does not understand Einstein's special theory of relativity. $E=mc^2$ is a thing of beauty but his time theory is not a constant thing....

KEYPAD

7	8	9
4	5	6
1	2	3
0		

1	2	3
4	5	6
7	8	9
	0	

Someone is trying to drive us crazy!

LAWS AND MAXIMS

Ms. Donne's Law: Never trust a man whose parents named him John, unless he has a sense of humor, and even then be careful.

Ms. Dylan's Law: Money doesn't talk, it curses.

Ms. Jagger-Richards' Law: Sometimes you get what you want, but you don't always get what you need.

Ms. Lombardi's Law: Timing isn't everything, but it's a lot.

Ms. Lullaby's Law: The hand that breaks the bough rules the world.

Ms. Machiavelli's Law: The means applied coerce the ends.

Ms. Murphy's Law: If anything can go wrong it will, unless you are in an adversarial situation and Murphy's Law is operating on the other side. In that case, if anything can go right, it will.

Ms. Peter's Law: Play expands to fill the time available; work is never finished.

Ms. F. Roosevelt's Law: We have the unknown to fear, and we do.

Ms. T. Roosevelt's Law: Speak softly and carry a big carrot.

Ms. Sherman's Law: Harmony is heaven, boys.

Ms. Williams's Law: Praise the Lord, and get out of doors during the daylight hours.

MISSION POSSIBLE

Life, as we know it on planet Earth, is corporeal, discrete, and transitory. Our source of creation is ethereal, inseparable, and eternal. And unable to lift heavy objects.

It is a question often asked, "If God is good, why does 'He' allow evil to exist in the world?" I have the answer. God has orders God must follow. God's ability to perform miracles is extremely limited. God is bound by all the degrees of nature. Just a second! Decrees of nature. For example, God cannot defy the law of gravity. Furthermore, the natural universe cannot produce "her" most beneficial effects without also producing potentially lethal effects. I do not refer to the mere existence of mortality but to powerfully energetic phenomena such as fire, radiation, and stormy weather. Our mission, should we decide to accept it, is to eliminate untimely deaths and other atrocities.

Even if one feels compelled to envision God as a being rather than another kind of entity, we, the people, still have the same mission. The only way for a "good" God to have "His" way in this world is to work through living instruments, because power corrupts beings and omnipotence would corrupt all-powerfully. Sophistry has its uses.

In either case, a paradise earned is more valued than a paradise endowed.

There is an alternative theory on the origin of all misfortune, which is: God has an evil twin; this twin stirs up suffering and "makes us do" bad deeds. Such a concept is cogent only in the minds of scienphobic humans. (Whoever is responsible for passing out high school diplomas in these United States has some explaining to do.) Picture this: the devil in his fireproof underwear, with a pitchfork in one hand and a Colt 45 in the other, threatening some poor sucker with the boredom of heaven. A terrific motivator, not.

God needs you. Neigh! Hi-yo, Silver, away! God needs us to finish and polish his work in the temporal realm. He/she/it/they can't do it without *homo sapiens*. We can comply with God in our mind. We should and we will overcome. Think hopefully; feel positively; act affirmatively. Drum roll, please! Exit singing, "This land is your land, this land is my land, from sea to shining sea, from the halls of Montezuma to the shores of Tripoli, this globe was left to you and me, and them. *Je t'aime*."

NUTRITION

Compare and contrast pandas and people, *homo sapiens!*

Pandas and people are both land mammals.

People are a highly evolved species; pandas are not. Pandas do not breed well in captivity. Humans breed almost anywhere. But one of the most significant things about pandas is that all pandas eat only one kind of food and the food is the same for each individual, a particular type of bamboo. Pandas are going to become extinct when something happens to that bamboo, assuming that they haven't already vanished due to overpopulation of humans in China (unless someone has developed an artificial panda food). Most, if not all, human individuals, on the other hand, need a variety of foods in their diet. But also I would expect to find that different groups of *homo sapiens* each thrive on different combinations of nutrients. So, if one particular food or class of foods becomes unavailable, while some groups will suffer illness and death, one or more other groups will survive and produce healthy offspring.

We are faced with a great difficulty in determining what is a good diet or a bad diet for each group or individual. Why? Because it seems to vary greatly from individual to individual, except, I suppose, for very inbred populations. A person needs varying kinds and amounts of vitamins and minerals to properly digest and utilize the different kinds of fat, protein, and carbohydrate-containing foods people can eat. What you need to eat depends in part on what else you are eating. And of course if you engage in lots of physical activity you need additional energy. Also, it is advisable to eat for the weather and climate. But a lot of the requirements for an individual's diet are in the genes. They have to be in the genes.

Have we not all heard stories of people who ate a diet high in saturated fats all their lives and lived to be one hundred years of age? If these stories are true, their longevity is primarily due to their "choice" of parents. Because many Americans who have followed such a diet have died or will die of heart disease.

Researchers may in time be able to tell us that our specific genes require x amounts of y nutrients over a certain period of time for good health. At present the research I have read about concerning heredity and diet is being done with obese people. One example is "A unique genetic heritage that for centuries enabled Pima Indians to survive in the harsh Southwest deserts is now endangering their health,…"

"'Their bodies seem to have developed a "thrifty gene" that stored fat during periods of feast so they could survive the famines,'" said Eric Ravussin, a Swiss physiologist who has been studying obesity among the Pima since 1984. When their diet consisted mainly of corn, beans, squash and some game, the 'thrifty gene' was an advantage. Now that food is plentiful the same gene "appears to be the main culprit in the 80 percent obesity rate among the Pimas.…[1]

Perhaps each person's optimum diet is not as individual as fingerprints. Most present-day Americans, however, have comparatively recent ancestors whose countries of origin are located in diverse locations on our planet and, furthermore, many have ancestors from more than one of those diverse locations. Therefore, U.S. residents have a special problem with Recommended Daily Allowances of this and that which do not take into consideration ethnic genetic differences regarding metabolism.

The mechanisms in the human body for dealing with excesses and deficiencies of various nutrients work only up to a point. Of course, some substitutions can be made. You don't have to eat all the nutrients you need in the correct proportions every day. But if all the people in the world ate an identical, supposedly well-balanced diet, a lot of them would be sick, ill, in poor health. I think.

Perhaps you agree with that statement but you also think that people have enough common sense and sense of taste to choose the foods they eat so that their diet, provided they have the necessary economic resources, will be appropriate for their own bodies and lifestyles. They don't.

"…as early as age two, social forces begin to influence eating and can eventually lead to quirky food preferences. Parents, inadvertently, are often the cause."

"The findings are part of a body of research indicating that psychological and social factors play a larger role than had been thought in determining a person's choice of foods, but that, even so, biology sometimes confounds people's best intentions, particularly when it comes to trying to lose weight."[2]

Whether people are consuming the wrong foods because they are trying to follow a diet designed for every person or because they eat the most convenient foods available or because they eat the foods they have been socialized

---

[1]Lori Zubalik, "Expert says Pima fat trait puts their health at risk," *Detroit Free Press* (Sept. 25, 1989), sec. B, p. 14.
[2]Daniel Goleman, "We Eat What We Are," *Detroit Free Press* (July 18, 1989), sec. C, p. 2.

to think are the most delicious or because they suffer economic deprivation, they will *still be ill* if their diets results in nutritional deficiencies or excesses. Did I leave out any adult reasons? No matter. People will still be ill if their diet results in nutritional deficiencies or excesses.

Oliver Alabaster, M.D., states "After years of studying diet in terms of deficiencies, scientists have recently come to realize something of immense importance: diseases can arise from an abundant and apparently normal diet, consumed over many years![3]

For those of you who think a sparse diet is the answer for everyone, consider this from the *Dictionary of Nutrition*. "The chief ingredients of the macrobiotic diet are grains and cereals, especially unpolished rice. Certain vegetables, seafood, nuts and seeds are included..." "Some persons in this country have apparently thrived on this diet. Others have gotten very sick, and some have died."[4]

George Watson, Ph.D., divides people into four "psychochemical types": slow oxidizers; fast oxidizers; normal oxidizers; and suboxidizers, depending on how rapidly each type burns carbohydrates to produce energy in cooperation with fats and proteins, particularly energy need to prevent impaired functioning of the brain. His theories are explained in detail in his book, *Nutrition and Your Mind*. "It is generally agreed that it is impossible to specify an ideal diet which applies to everyone."[5]

Fast oxidizers need more fats and proteins, particularly high purine proteins, and less carbohydrates than people with normal metabolisms, along with increased amounts of vitamins A, E, B_{12}, niacinamide, calcium pantothenate, vitamin C, bioflavonoids, choline, inositol, calcium, phosphorus, iodine, and zinc sulfate.[6] On the other hand, the slow oxidizers need their proteins to be low in purines with comparatively less total fats and proteins and more carbohydrates. They benefit from increased amounts of vitamins B_1, B_2, B_6, para-aminobenzoic acid, niacin, ascorbic acid, vitamin D, potassium citrate, magnesium chloride, copper gluconate, manganese oxide, and ferrous sulfate.[7] Suboxidizers must avoid casual eating practices.[8] I take that to mean *no junk food*, ever.

---

[3]Oliver Alabaster, M.D., *What You Can Do To prevent Cancer.* (New York, Simon and Schuster, 1985), p. 32.

[4]Richard Ashley and Heidi Duggal, *Dictionary of Nutrition* (New York, Pocket Books, 1976), p. 123.

[5]George Watson, *Nutrition and Your Mind* (New York, Bantam Books, 1974), p. 124.

[6]Ibid., pp. 116-118.

[7]Ibid., pp. 119-120.

[8]Ibid., pp. 125.

Even if many American didn't ingest too much fat, refined sugar, and salt, probably regardless of their psychochemical type, one can see many opportunities for biochemical mischief if a person of one psychochemical type follows a diet designed for another psychochemical type. Watson is concerned with so-called mental illness without a sound psychological cause. "The failure to distinguish between psychochemical behavior and motivated, meaningful behavior is at the bottom of the chaos in psychotherapy."[9] But I suspect "physical" illnesses also do occur if one follows the wrong "oxidizer" diet.

A WARNING FOR THE INTERESTED READER: The medieval theory of humours also depended upon dividing people into four mental health types. "Choler, which was related to the element fire, made a man wrathful; blood, related to the element air, made him sanguine and over-optimistic; phlegm, related to water, made him silent and morose; and melancholy, related to earth, made him despondent."[10] Need I say this medieval theory has been discredited?

The author of *Diet for a Small Planet,* Frances Moore Lappe, refers to an article by R.W. Williams ("We Abnormal Normals," *Nutrition Today,* 2:19-23, 1967) in writing on protein individuality. "He points out that if beef were the only source of protein, one person's minimum needs could be met by two ounces of meat; yet another individual might require eight ounces. Although over 98 percent of a population may not range more than 30 percent from an average requirement, these two possible extremes represent a fourfold difference in protein requirement! And requirements for other nutrients are found to be equally, or even more widely, disparate."[11]

So much for generalities. I hope to show that ingesting nutrients which don't match your individual requirements causes certain classes of diseases.

There was a segment on the TV show *20/20* in 1989 which warned that people were getting lead poisoning from pottery dishes. Most of the improperly fired pottery was manufactured outside the United States. However, we import it. The show was a reminder that minerals are toxic in large enough doses. In addition, balances between minerals have to be maintained in the human body.

"Phosphorus and calcium, though not chemically related, occur together in the body in an almost constant ratio of 1.5 to 1 (calcium to phosphorus).

---

[9] Ibid., p. 16.

[10] M. H. Abrams et al, *Norton Anthology of English Literature, Volume I* (New York, W.W. Norton & Company, Inc., 1962), p. 350.

[11] Frances Moore Lappe, *Diet for a Small Planet* (New York, Ballantine Books, Revised Edition 1975), p. 76.

But if the diet is too high in phosphorus in relation to calcium intake—and in many American diets this is the case—calcium is lost through the urine. And if the intake of calcium is inadequate, phosphorus is not properly absorbed and used."[12] In *The Vitamin Book* the authors write "...[phosphorus and calcium] act as barometers for each other to maintain a constant ratio. Every bone in the body contains calcium and phosphorous in a ratio of two to one, and interestingly, the same ratio is found in human breast milk."[13] Whatever the correct ratio may be, I contend there is one. And, of course, vitamin D in the correct proportion is also needed to help maintain the correct mineral balance.

Another example is the sodium-potassium balance. "The human body contains about three times as much potassium as sodium and good health requires that this balance be maintained. An excess of sodium causes potassium to be lost through the urine and an excess of potassium causes sodium to be lost."[14] "No RDA has been established for sodium or potassium, but it has been estimated that we need about 1,000 mg. of sodium a day (equivalent to 2,500 mg. of salt) and 2,000-6,000 mg. of potassium."[15]

I have not read of any other constant mineral ratios but I have read about other excessive intakes of one mineral causing deficiencies in others.

"High zinc intakes can decrease absorption of iron and copper...." "Calcium interferes with zinc absorption."[16] "Copper functions on a see-saw basis with molybdenum. If you have excess copper, your molybdenum level will drop, if you have excess molybdenum, your copper level will drop."[17] "...Iron, cadmium, and surprisingly, Vitamin C have been shown to decrease copper absorption."[18] At the same time, "Anemia is a major symptom of copper deficiency, and this is because copper is so necessary for iron to be absorbed, transported, and utilized."[19] I really, really suppose there are many other mineral interactions in the human body due to the inappropriate combinations of foods, and possibly mineral supplements, one consumes (interactions as present not known to me) which produce abnormal proportional relationships of minerals in the body.

Should we be troubled by abnormal proportional relationships of minerals in our bodies? "Scientists who have studied the effects of diet and cancer have

---

[12]Ashley and Duggal, *op. cit.*, p. 153.
[13]Harold M. Silverman, Pharm. D., Joseph A. Romano, *Pharm.D.*, and Gary Elmer, Ph.D., *The Vitamin Book* (New York, Bantam Books, 1986), p. 218.
[14]Ashley and Duggal, *op. cit.*, p. 200.
[15]Silverman, Romano and Elmer, *op. cit.*, p. 264.
[16]Ibid., pp. 239-240.
[17]Ibid., p. 244.
[18]Ibid., p. 246.
[19]Ibid., p. 247.

found that about 60% of cancer in women and 40% of cancer in men could be due to dietary factors."[20] That sentence clearly does not state that consuming excessive amounts of fats and substances like nitrates, which are considered to be carcinogens, are the only dietary factors involved in the production of cancers we need be concerned about.

May I have your attention?

There is a gland in the human body which enlarges in the presence of a scarcity of iodine. An overgrowth of normal thyroid tissue is called goiter and is common among people with a very low intake of iodine. I had something different when I was a young adult, a "cold" thyroid growth, i.e., an enlargement that did not absorb radioactive (or any other) iodine. I was told, after a successful bilateral thyroidectomy, that the tumor—diagnosed as a carcinoma—was very similar to normal thyroid tissue. Further, there are some thyroid tumors that are so like thyroid tissue they even produce thyroid hormone. I was not told the probable cause of my tumor and I had never, that I knew of, been exposed to large amounts of radiation.

So I asked myself why my body would create thyroid tissue, named cancer or not, that was not capable of containing iodine. Because the presence of a superabundance of iodine in my body was interfering with the proper functioning of such a chemically dependent gland was my answer. I thought that a gland that could become larger with an iodine deficiency could be programmed to reduce the density of iodine in the total thyroid area by growing a part that would hold zero iodine. An alternative answer was that my body was having to make do with too little iodine but, before my theorizing, I had habitually used lots of iodized salt.

The scientific empirical evidence is starting to come in. This statement appears in a book first published in 1985: "There is evidence that excess amounts and low amounts of iodine can each predispose you to a different type of thyroid cancer."[21] I expect it to be known in my lifetime if the type of tumor I had is the result of an excess of iodine relative to certain other nutrients, or if it is not.

The more interesting question, of course, is, if the thyroid reacts to a mineral excess or deficiency by growing "cancer" cells, why can't other body tissues do the same? We shouldn't think that they cannot because cancer is a DISEASE and diseases are caused by viruses or bacteria or defective genes. Scurvy is a disease. Likewise beriberi. Moreover, "Some (cancer cells) look very much

---

[20]Alabaster, *op. cit.*, p. 13,
[21]Ibid., p. 175

like the healthy cells around them…"[22] The term "Differentiation in cancer cells means that they still act like the normal cells from which they grew."[23] These nearly normal cells may have different causes than severely malignant cancers. Additionally, nutritional involvement is a possible explanation for "spontaneous" remissions.

The biochemistry of the human body, I suppose, is too complex for the complete cause of any category of cancer to be such a simple thing as the ingestion of an excess or deficiency of one mineral (with respect to the amount required by a person's metabolism) but, what if one group of people's average daily need for iodine is four times as much as a second group of people's daily need for iodine and other persons' needs are somewhere in between, and furthermore, a group of people's RDA for iron ought to be four times as much as another group of people's RDA for iron ought to be and again the remaining people's needs for iron are somewhere is between and their diet provides all of them with about the same amount of these substances? Assuming that the individual people in iodine group I may or may not be in iron group A or in iron group Z or in any of the middle classifications as long as each one fits in somewhere. The same for iodine group (i). Is this getting too complicated? Et cetera for some other minerals and vitamins.

Until it has been disproved that the balance of minerals consumed by a particular human being has no causal relationship (on the cause side—not the effect side) with the development of any of the diseases named cancers, I think it safer to assume that the abnormal proportional relationships of minerals do exist and can be hazardous to your health.

When I wrote about individual requirements for minerals and used iron as an example, did you think I picked it at random?

When "Over 80 percent of the iodine in the human body can be found in the thyroid gland,…"[24] and "Of the iron in the body, 60-70 percent is stored in hemoglobin, the red part of red blood cells."[25] are both true, it seems to me worthwhile looking for parallels in the appearance of iron and iodine in the human body.

Both minerals are necessary for important functions to be performed by the gland and cells that contain the greatest amounts of them. The thyroid uses iodine to produce thyroid hormones that regulate the body's metabolism

---

[22]Kathryn H. Salsbury and Eleanor Liebman Johnson, *The Indispensable Cancer Handbook* (New York, Seaview Book, 1981), p. 6.
[23]Ibid., p. 16.
[24]Silverman, Romano and Elmer, *op. cit.*, p. 226.
[25]Ibid., p. 230.

and hemoglobin carries oxygen from the lungs to body tissues. Just as there is a common iodine deficiency disease, there is a common iron deficiency disease—anemia (hypochromic microcytic anemia). "The red blood cells become smaller than normal and pale in color due to the lack of iron in the hemoglobin."[26] This shows a direct change of production in the quality of red blood cells, although perhaps not in the quantity. I suspect there can be changes in the quantity of red blood cells due to the presence of a scarcity of iron or a superabundance of iron also, similar in some respects to the changes of quantity that occur with thyroid tissue.

There ought to be evidence to be found that excess amounts and low amounts of iron can each predispose you to a different type of leukemia.

"Leukemias do not usually show up in the form of tumors, but rather are characterized by the production of enormous numbers of white blood cells, which never reach maturity and cannot do the regular work of healthy cells."[27] White blood cells, at least normal mature ones, are not identical to red blood cells without hemoglobin and therefore without four atoms of iron included in a normal hemoglobin protein, but I would like to point out that if the human body produced "red" blood cells that did not contain hemoglobin, they would be white blood cells. Is this possible?

"Most blood cells are produced in the bone marrow (perhaps 2 percent are produced in the spleen)."[28] From the same source, "Medical scientists now believe that all types of blood cells are derived from a common ancestor, called a pluripotent stem cell...." "In appearance, stem cells resemble young lymphocytes (a type of leukocyte)...."[29] Leukocyte means white blood cell. Therefore, the parent cells of red blood cells are immature "white" blood cells. Further, leukemia cells are not easily classified by appearance as to the type of abnormal white cell they are; one source writes, referring to leukemia cells, "Microscopic examination of white blood cells has proven to be a very inexact means of identification."[30]

I suggest this means production can be switched from one type of blood cell to another very easily regardless of the "color" of those blood cells. Researchers think "...red blood cells are not of major conceptual importance in

---

[26]Ibid, p. 232.
[27]Salsbury and Johnson, *op. cit.*, p. 242.
[28]Cynthia P. Margolies and Kenneth B. McCredie, M.D., *Understanding Leukemia* (New York, Charles Scribner's Sons, 1983), p. 5.
[29]Ibid., p. 7.
[30]Ibid., p. 10.
[31]Ibid., p. 8.

relation to leukemia in that they are not part of the immune-response system"[31] I think they should be of conceptual importance. The amount of iron absorbed by the human body varies greatly depending upon circumstances. "It has been estimated that, on an average, only about 10 percent of food iron is absorbed, although this can increase to 20 percent if the body's iron stores are low."[32] A person, especially a pregnant person, may not eat enough iron-containing foods following a normal diet plan to satisfy his requirement for iron even with a higher absorption rate. On the other hand, a person who ingests large amounts of iron can easily accumulate too much because "Unlike other nutrient metals, iron cannot be excreted."[33]

Leukemia might be held in check by a properly functioning immune system which is supposedly impossible because white blood cells—some of which are non-functioning with leukemia—are so critical to it; but since anemia can accompany leukemia ("Suspicious findings include low levels of hemoglobin or a low red blood count…"[34]), when these conditions occur together, why not consider them part of one disease process?

Is anybody out there asking, "What about viruses?" It is stated in *Understanding Leukemia* that "It has recently been demonstrated that transmissible viruses are strongly implicated in the majority of malignant tumors in animals, and in animal leukemia."[35] Viruses can change RNA and DNA segments. The authors also report that most scientists believe that cancer develops in two steps.[36] "A sizable group among cancer researchers goes even further: maintaining that although the inductive event can be a genetic abnormality that is either inherited or acquired, the promotional event is always acquired, such as exposure to carcinogens."[37] Is this material out of date? If you will allow me to declare that a disproportionate amount of iron in the human body can be an acquired event, I will allow you to declare that viruses must change genetic coding in order for certain non-inherited disease processes to develop.

There is a group of diseases, besides cancers, which are sometimes associated with viruses, sometimes with a "failure" of the immune system, sometimes with a chemical problem, and sometimes with body damage from an outside force although in this case the damage is due to an injury to a joint

---

[32]Silverman, Romano and Elmer, *op. cir.*, p. 232.
[33]Better Homes and Gardens, *New Family Medical Guide*, edited by Edwin Kieser, Jr. (Des Moines, Meredith Corp., 1982), p. 98.
[34]Margolies and McCredie, *op. cit.*, p. 23.
[35]Ibid., p. 43.
[36]Ibid., pp. 73 and 74.
[37]Ibid., p. 74.

rather than due to cell damage from radiation. (I hope I don't now have to quote authorities to show radiation can lead to cancer.) I refer to a group of diseases called rheumatic diseases, among them various types of arthritis.

Here is evidence that joint damage is a cause of some arthritis. "Osteoarthritis is often considered to be the result of years of normal wear and tear on joints, but can also develop after damage to a joint from injury or infection."[38] Testimony regarding involvement of viruses is this quote from *Arthritis and Rheumatism: The Facts:* "For example, a number of known viruses, such as rubella (German measles) can cause an arthritis which invariably clears completely..."[39] At present most researchers think only one kind of rheumatic disease is the result of a chemical problem. "[Gout] is caused essentially by hyperuricaemia, an excess of uric acid in the blood and tissues."[40]

I think if there is one disease classified as rheumatic that can partially be treated by a change in diet, there can be others. As to immune system involvement in arthritis, "In many forms of arthritis, however, the inflammatory process goes out of control; it doesn't subside when it should, and leads to further tissue damage rather than tissue repair."[41] In particular, rheumatoid arthritis is thought to be an autoimmune disease "...implying an abnormal immune reaction directed against some body component..."[42] and to further emphasize the possibility that something that naturally occurs in the human body such as a mineral is a factor in rheumatoid arthritis: "The immune system errs at some point and mistakenly attacks normal tissues as if they were antigens."[43]

Because these kinds of comparisons can be made between cancers and rheumatic diseases, and since diet *is* so important in cancer prevention, it is likely that diet will be found to be important in arthritis prevention also. I know current medical thinking says no, but to reiterate, I don't think individual nutritional requirements and the possibility of nutrient imbalances on a normal diet have been taken into account.

There as been so much research about the disease process in rheumatoid arthritis, I am able to suggest a candidate for a "mineral excess" factor. "[Rheumatoid arthritis] is a chronic disorder, developing over months or years, involving essentially the synovial joints of the body. The synovial membrane

---

[38]Arthritis Foundation, Editor Irving Kushner, M.D., Associate Editors Ann Forer and Ann B. McGuire, *Understanding Arthritis* (New York, Charles Scribner's Sons, 1984), p. 5.
[39]J. T. Scott, M.D., *Arthritis and Rheumatism: The Facts* (Oxford, Oxford University Press, 1980), p. 22.
[40]Ibid., p. 68.
[41]Kushner, *op. cit.,* pp. 12 and 13.
[42]Scott, *op. cit.,* p. 26.
[43]Kushner, *op. cit.,* p. 15.

becomes inflamed and swollen, and infiltrated by inflammatory cells."[44] This mineral excess may not be the initial "triggering event" but consider this description from an earlier book on arthritis. "Complexes—the bound combinations of enemy agent, antibody, and complement—are swallowed up by eating cells, as they should be. But for some reason not yet understood, the complexes prove to be the more than the eating cell can handle. Some of its enzymes escape from their sacs and the cell 'vomits' them out into the surrounding fluid— the fluid of the joint."[45] Nothing may flash into your mind when you read that but something flashed into mine after one reading. "That's bleach—chlorine!"

Do I expect you to believe bleach exists in the human body? Yes. Dr. Peter Gott wrote about recent research on the immune system in one of his medical columns "...when combined with the hydrogen peroxide excreted by macrophages (and by neutrophils themselves), a violent chemical reaction ensues. The bonding of myeloperoxidase and hydrogen peroxide produces hypochlorous acid, which readily destroys bacteria.

"WHY IS this reaction so interesting?

"Because hypochlorous acid is the sole active ingredient in liquid household bleach,"[46] It is true that Dr. Gott also says in his article that this acid causes no damage to normal human tissues. May I suggest that this statement is not precisely accurate? Bottles of household bleach commonly carry a warning such as "WILL IRRITATE SKIN AND EYES. HARMFUL IF SWALLOWED." Maybe there are some internal cells that are also irritated.

The primary reason I wonder if chlorine should be investigated as a factor in rheumatoid arthritis is because there is an ancient theory (or superstition) that wearing copper jewelry will cure arthritis. Why? "...metallic copper is not absorbed through the skin..."[47] Even if it were, people with rheumatoid arthritis probably wouldn't be helped by that happening because "[nutritionists and other scientists] have been especially interested in copper, and have found that the amounts of this metal in the blood and joint fluid are higher in people who have rheumatoid arthritis than in normal people.:[48] An early study showed three times as much in joint fluid.[49]

---

[44]Scott, op. cit., p. 20.

[45]Darrell C. Crain, M.D., *The Arthritis Handbook* (New York, Arco Publishing Company, Inc., 1971), p. 34.

[46]Peter Gott, M.D., "Microscopic battle constantly fought inside our bodies to control health," *The Flint Journal* (Sept. 24, 1989).

[47]John J. Calabro, M.D. and John Wykert, *The Truth about Arthritis Care* (Hardcover edition, 1971), p. 215.

[48]Kushner, *op. cit.*, p. 104.

[49]Calabro and Wykert, *op. cit.*, p. 215.

However, *chloride can leave the body* through the skin. At least I assume that when people perspire they lose sodium chloride as well as other salts. Copper on the outside of human skin may pull chloride inside the body out. In other words, a chemical reaction occurs that results in external copper chloride. Has any one shown there are not lots of chloride ions in the synovial joint fluid of RA patients? Too many? "Sodium and potassium exist in and around cells as 'ions' with a plus charge."[50] "The usual 'counter ion' with a negative charge is chloride (from chlorine)."[51] Another reason for suspecting mineral involvement in RA is because "Injections of gold salts (gold sodium thiomalate, trade name Myochrysine, and aurothioglucose, trade name Solganol) have been used to treat rheumatoid arthritis for more than fifty years."[52] Wouldn't gold salts react more readily with chloride than with white blood cells? Also, techniques (such as steam baths) to produce sweating have been used for centuries in various parts of the world to treat arthritis.[53]

Medical researchers have been trying for a long time to find the elusive "virus" that causes rheumatoid arthritis and haven't yet been successful. Of course, they haven't yet been successful in finding a connection between diet and RA either. I suspect the reason is that all the subjects in a research study are expected to develop a particular type of arthritis when they follow similar diets. It doesn't work that way. But please note "People with severe rheumatoid arthritis often do have nutritional abnormalities such as low levels of certain vitamins and minerals in their blood and tissues. These abnormalities are results rather than causes of the disease because the same abnormalities are found in other diseases characterized by chronic inflammation."[54] If I can disagree with the statement that red blood cells are not of conceptual importance in leukemia, I can also disagree with the last sentence quoted. And I do. Ought we to be so sure which is cause and which is effect, particularly when low levels of some nutrients are accompanied by high levels of others?

In any event, I am convinced that one's diet has more to do with the state of a person's health than both the medical professionals and the general public are prepared to accept at present. Because of metabolic individuality. Because most of us have our very own quantity requirements for all the nutrients a human being needs. May I be excused for not attempting to list them all?

---

[50]Silverman, Romano and Elmer, *op. cit.*, p. 263.
[51]Ibid., p. 264.
[52]Kushner, *op. cit.*, p. 56.
[53]Bernard Aschner, M.D., *Arthritis Can Be Cured* (New York, Arc Books, Inc., 1968), pages on the history of medicine.
[54]Kushner, *op. cit.*, p. 102.

I would like medical researchers to design studies to test for relationships between mineral imbalances and cancers and for relationships between mineral imbalances and rheumatic diseases, but that may not happen even in the twenty-first century. Also, there is the possibility that there no relationship whatsoever between mineral imbalances and the aforesaid classes of diseases. But there are causes somewhere to be found. And when causes are found, *sometimes* diseases can be prevented or cured. Wouldn't that be wonderful?

OUR HELP[1]

O God, our help in ages past,
Our hope for years to come,
Our shelter from the killing blast,
And our eternal home!

Under the brightness of thy sun
Still may we dwell secure;
Forever is the battle won,
So we may long endure.

Before the hills in order stood,
Or earth received her frame,
From everlasting thou were Good,
To endless time the same.

A thousand seasons, in thy sight,
Are like a moment run;
Short as the watch that ends the night,
Before the rising sun.

O God, our help in ages past,
Our hope for years to come;
Be thou our guide while life shall last,
And our eternal home!

---

[1]Slightly revised version of "O God, Our Help in Ages Past," Isaac Watts

PRESCRIPTION

Why is it not general practice to pay firemen according to the number of fires they attempt to put out? Or policemen according to the number of crimes they investigate? Because those firemen, or policemen, would have no positive financial incentives to prevent fires or crimes. And as someone once said, "An ounce of prevention is worth a pound of cure." Likewise, physicians, in a traditional fee for service pay scheme, earn most of their livelihood when their patients are ill or injured. In other words, in years past, your friendly family doctor was not being paid to keep you healthy. If he was human, and he probably was, he saw himself as a healer and not a wellness counselor. It was the system.

Well, the system needs to be changed. And not by putting every American into a health maintenance organization for health care needs. What's wrong with American HMOs? Generally, they are for-profit corporations. Generally, they deny their patients a second opinion if the primary care physician is of the opinion patients can do without a specialist. But worse of all, they do not routinely pay in dollars for their mistakes. If an HMO saves money by denying expensive care to a patient who doesn't need it, in all fairness it ought to have to pay a financial penalty when it denied care to a patient who did need it and would have been known to need it (by a competent doctor). Whether the decision constituted malpractice or not, the patient, the patient's next health care provider, or the patient's next of kin is owed for all benefits covered by the contract.

If not HMOs, then what?

I think you already know. A public health service. But not a public health service organization that includes the entire American health care system. The public health service would provide primary care physician-wellness counselor-specialist resource allocation expert teams in numbers as needed. Those health care practitioners would be on government salaries. Free-market specialists would do everything else on a fee for service basis paid by a government program for all those who wish to be enrolled. Rah! Rah! Rah! Single payer, single payer! Yeah! Yeah! Yeah! The public health service teams would decide where the patients go for medical treatment and tests. The specialist resource allocation expert would be the informed "consumer" doing cost-benefit analysis.

Each primary care doctor would have a yearly budget based on number of patients and their prior medical history to spend. Total medical budgets for each fiscal year will be apportioned to the states by Congress according to the number enrolled and funds available.

When all else fails, ask the patient.

If it ain't broke, do regular maintenance.

If life hands you a lemon, make yourself a nice cup of tea and drop the slices in.

QUIZ

A reading diversion.

Question:	Hint:
Who is the big cheese of the greatest rock and roll band in the world?	I like that old time rock and roll. That kind of music just soothes my soul.
The blue king?	I know who I love, But the devil knows who I'll marry.
The lead guitarist?	Oh, the preacher went down to the cellar to pray. He found a jug and he stayed all day.
The closet romantic?	Christ, if my love were in my arms, and I in my bed again.
The occasional pianist?	Rain, rain, go away! Come again some other day.
The constant dreamer?	Roses love sunshine, violets love dew, Angels in heaven know I love you.
The universal voice?	I see London, I see France; I see someone's underpants.
The soldier queen?	Words, words, words! I'm so sick of words. I get words all day long, first from him, now from you.

The crafty ghost?	I ain't goin' to study war no more, down by the riverside.
The retired mystic?	If not for you, I couldn't hear a robin sing.
The chief consoler?	She turned into a lover and, mother, what a lover.
The proper ethicist?	It is the dawning of the Age of Aquarius.

Straightforward questions, eh? Clues to the only absolutely correct answers are on another page of this book. Further, none of these people is St. Elvis the Baptist.

RE: SURNAMES

It has regretfully become necessary to change the American conventions regarding surnames in order to keep children whose parents have divorced and married other people or whose parents never married from being segregated on account of their lack of one "family" name. Don't ask/don't tell: "Are your parents married?"

The new customs are: children take their mothers' surname; women do not change their names upon marriage or divorce; men change theirs upon marriage only socially and, perhaps, when filling out government forms. The social change doesn't survive the marriage. Because I said so.

An adult male and adult female are Mr. Bob Bachelor and Ms. Jane Joyful when marital status is irrelevant. They become Mas Bob Bachelor and Miss Jane Joyful when marital status is pertinent and they are single. As a couple married to each other, she gets the missus and he gets the change in name. Here are Mr. Bob Joyful and Mrs. Jane Joyful. It was time for a change,

To address a formal non-business letter to the couple, use Mr. Robert and Mrs. Jane Joyful with the salutation Mr. and Mrs. Joyful. Their preteen children are Master Richard Joyful and Young Miss Mary Joyful, or Dick and Mary. Their teenage children are never at home and only want letters from their peers so they need not be addressed at all. I am nothing if not logical. And don't you forget it.

SCHOOL DAYS

"School's out, school's out, teacher's let the fools out!" translated means summer vacation is here. But Mr. Studies has proved most first grade through senior year in high school students would retain more knowledge from each school year if their summer vacations were shorter. Perhaps we could eliminate the fools from our schools all year round by cutting out those well loved summer vacations. Drastic but necessary surgery. How to make it work? Most teachers don't want to work more days per year without a raise in pay. The state of Michigan wants to improve education for its children without an increase in the costs for schools. In 1995, most Michigan public school districts had 180 days of classes, meeting Monday thru Friday most weeks, and at least two consecutive months of down time in the summer. Situation hopeless? No. Why not change the public school schedules so that children attend teaching classes only on Monday, Tuesday, Thursday, and Friday? Wednesday would be another study day at home, in libraries or in study halls supervised by adults without teaching certificates. We would have 176 days of instruction, fewer than currently, in 44 weeks. That leaves eight weeks to be divided among summer, fall, winter, and spring vacations set up by the school districts. Isn't math wonderful? In addition, another two weeks of semi-vacation time for each student while school is in session could be permitted for the convenience of families and the tourist industry, with the school work to be made up before, during, and after the individually scheduled vacations.

TAXES

I hereby propose replacing national income taxes with money or monetary estimate transfer taxes. Yes! That will be M.O.M.E.T. Tax for short. Now who wouldn't love a tax that combines the word *mom* with the appealing E.T.? The M.O.M.E.T. Tax will be equitable. A good mom is always fair. And the M.O.M.E.T. Tax will be calculated on one diminutive form. As easy as riding a single-speed bicycle once you learn how, I promise. 'Twill be easy except for writing the check or equivalent *to pay the tax*. Why should that little difficulty stop this wonderful concept? I am not ashamed to borrow good ideas. Retain the withholding procedure on wages or salaries paid. Banks can withhold estimated taxes on other money transfers of which they have knowledge. If you inferred from that last sentence that monetary transfers not now considered to be income will be taxed, you inferred correctly. In exchange, there will be lower tax rates for most of us and simple tax calculations. K.I.S.S.

The federal "graduated" income tax rates, for real rather than corporate persons, in effect as this book is being written are sporadically, rather than gradually, increased as one's income subject to tax increases (one year was 15%/28%/33%). Furthermore, the Social Security tax is an additional hefty flat rate tax on incomes. The result is a mad scramble to persuade the U.S. Congress to allow deductions from gross income (or provide income tax credits) that benefit you and me, but not them. The United States government could collect just as much in income taxes with a simplified tax code that elevates the tax rates in increments of 1 percent and in the process throw some of our hard-working tax attorneys and accountants into other professions. I don't like to think of what these other professions might be, but there are always tradeoffs. K.I.S.S.

What, precisely, do I have in mind? I have in mind a linear relationship between total in-coming funds subject to tax and the applicable tax rates. Straight, straight, straight line, line, line on a graph, graph, graph. K.I.S.S.

Before I proceed, please allow me to convince you that a flat rate income tax is not as linear as you think it is. Let assume a 20 percent flat rate tax on incomes. Oh, come on. If one allows personal exemptions and/or standard deductions and/or minimum income not subject to tax to be subtracted from gross income, that means, in effect, one's income from $0.00 up to the total amount subtracted (for example, $5,000) is taxed at 0 percent and one's income from $5,000 (or whatever) on up is taxed at 20 percent. Draw both those relationships on a graph and you will get a line with a 90 degree angle in it, part vertical and part horizontal. That does not constitute a straight line where I come from. K.I.S.S.

A flat-rate income tax rate is only linear if it kicks in on the first $1.00 of actual income. Say I. And collecting that 20 cents (or x cents) on the dollar if the cost of filing a tax return was more than a person's total income for the year would be very, very tricky. It might even be unconstitutional. K.I.S.S.

My proposal avoids that problem just mentioned. Of course, it creates others. Let me give you a for instance. For instance, the bracket amount could be $10,000. If the total amount subject to the M.O.M.E.T. Tax is from $0-$9,999, the tax rate is 0 percent. If the total amount subject to the M.O.M.E.T. Tax is from $10,000-$19,999, the tax rate is 1 percent. If the total amount subject to the M.O.M.E.T. Tax is from $20,000-$29,999, the tax rate is 2 percent. If the total amount subject to the M.O.M.E.T. Tax is from $30,000-$39,999, the tax rate is 3 percent. If the total amount subject to the M.O.M.E.T. Tax is from $40,000-$49,999, the tax rate is 4 percent. If the total amount subject to the M.O.M.E.T. Tax is from $50,000-$59,999, the tax rate is 5 percent. If the total amount subject to the M.O.M.E.T. Tax is from $60,000-$69,999, the tax rate is 6 percent. If the total amount subject to the M.O.M.E.T. Tax is from $70,000-$79,999, the tax rate is 7 percent. If the total amount subject to the M.O.M.E.T. Tax is from $80,000-$89,999, the tax rate is 8 percent. If the total amount subject to the M.O.M.E.T. Tax is from $90,000-$99,999, the tax rate is 9 percent.

I can keep this up if you can. If the total amount subject to the M.O.M.E.T. Tax is from $100,000-$109,999, the tax rate is 10 percent. If the total amount subject to the M.O.M.E.T. Tax is from $110,000-$119,999, the tax rate is 11 percent. If the total amount subject to the M.O.M.E.T. Tax is from $120,000-$129,999, the tax rate is 12 percent. If the total amount subject to the M.O.M.E.T. Tax is from $130,000-$139,999, the tax rate is 13 percent. If the total amount subject to the M.O.M.E.T. Tax is from $140,000-$149,999, the tax rate is 14 percent. If the total amount subject to the M.O.M.E.T. Tax is from $150,000-$159,999, the tax rate is 15 percent. If the total amount subject to the M.O.M.E.T. Tax is from $160,000-$169,999, the tax rate is 16 percent. Are you asleep yet? If the total amount subject to the M.O.M.E.T. Tax is from $170,000-$179,999, the tax rate is 17 percent. If the total amount subject to the M.O.M.E.T. Tax is from $180,000-$189,999, the tax rate is 18 percent. If the total amount subject to the M.O.M.E.T. Tax is from $190,000-$199,999, the tax rate is 19 percent.

If the total amount subject to the M.O.M.E.T. Tax is from $200,000-$209,999, the tax rate is 20 percent. If the total amount subject to the M.O.M.E.T. Tax is from $210,000-$219,999, the tax rate is 21 percent. If the total amount subject to the M.O.M.E.T. Tax is from $220,000-$229,999, the tax rate is 22 percent. *Roses are red.* If the total amount subject to the M.O.M.E.T. Tax is from $230,000-$239,999, the tax rate is 23 percent. If the total amount subject to the M.O.M.E.T. Tax is from $240,000-$249,999, the tax rate is 24 percent. If the total amount subject to the M.O.M.E.T. Tax is from $250,000-$259,999, the tax rate is 25 percent. If the total amount subject to the M.O.M.E.T. Tax is from $260,000-$269,999, the tax rate is 26 percent. *Violets are blue.* If the total amount subject to the M.O.M.E.T. Tax is from $270,000-$279,999, the tax rate is 27 percent. If the total amount subject to the M.O.M.E.T. Tax is from $280,000-$289,999, the tax rate is 28 percent. If the total amount subject to the M.O.M.E.T. Tax is from $290,000-$299,999, the tax rate is 29 percent.

If the total amount subject to the M.O.M.E.T. Tax is from $300,000-$309,999, the tax rate is 30 percent. *Kids have to be fed.* If the total amount subject to the M.O.M.E.T. Tax is from $310,000-$319,999, the tax rate is 31 percent. If the total amount subject to the M.O.M.E.T. Tax is from $320,000-$329,999, the tax rate is 32 percent. If the total amount subject to the M.O.M.E.T. Tax is from $330,000-$339,999, the tax rate is 33 percent. If the total amount subject to the M.O.M.E.T. Tax is from $340,000-$349,999, the tax rate is 34 percent. *And so do you.* If the total amount subject to the M.O.M.E.T. Tax is from $350,000-$359,999, the tax rate is 35 percent. If the total amount subject to the M.O.M.E.T. Tax is from $360,000-$369,999, the tax rate is 36 percent. Read this chapter to a friend. If the total amount subject to the M.O.M.E.T. Tax is from $370,000-$379,999, the tax rate is 37 percent. If the total amount subject to the M.O.M.E.T. Tax is from $380,000-$389,999, the tax rate is 38 percent. If the total amount subject to the M.O.M.E.T. Tax is from $390,000-$399,999, the tax rate is 39 percent.

If the total amount subject to the M.O.M.E.T. Tax is from $400,000-$409,999, the tax rate is 40 percent. *The whole thing.* If the total amount subject to the M.O.M.E.T. Tax is from $410,000-$419,999, the tax rate is 41 percent. If the total amount subject to the M.O.M.E.T. Tax is from $420,000-$429,999, the tax rate is 42 percent. If the total amount subject to the M.O.M.E.T. Tax is from $430,000-$439,999, the tax rate is 43 percent. If the total amount subject to the M.O.M.E.T. Tax is from $440,000-$449,999, the tax rate is 74 percent. *Just wanted to see if you were paying attention.* The tax rate is 44 percent. If the total amount subject to the M.O.M.E.T. Tax is from $450,000-$459,999, the tax rate is 45 percent. If the total amount subject to the M.O.M.E.T. Tax is from $460,000-$469,999, the tax rate is 46 percent. *My word processor made me do it.* If the total amount subject to the M.O.M.E.T. Tax is from $470,000-$479,999, the tax rate is 47 percent. If the total amount subject to the M.O.M.E.T. Tax is from $480,000-$489,999, the tax rate is 48 percent. If the total amount subject to the M.O.M.E.T. Tax is from $490,000-$499,999, the tax rate is 49 percent. If the total amount subject to the M.O.M.E.T. Tax is from $500,000-infinity the tax rate is 50 percent. K.I.S.S.

By setting the top tax rate at 50 percent, I have just lost the straight (slanted) line on a graph I was after. But not to a 90 degree turn. And I had to stop somewhere. My guess is a substantial majority of Americans would agree that an income tax rate in excess of 50 percent has moved from taxation to confiscation, and odds are the U.S. Supreme Court would find income tax rates of 101 percent and counting a tad excessive. K.I.S.S.

To a mathematical purist, I never had a straight line to begin with. I had a jagged slanted line because I did not have a beginning tax rate of .0001 percent on taxable income of $1.00, and so on and so forth. A tax scheme which required an understanding of the subject of calculus would not be as simple as I would wish. K.I.S.S.

I have the ghastly fear in my mind that a $10,000 bracket amount for real people would not raise enough revenue for the U.S. Government to maintain its current pace of expenditures. Not to worry. The U.S. Congress would have the responsibility of deciding the bracket amount each year. It might be higher than $10,000, resulting in lower taxes overall, or it might be lower than $10,000, resulting in higher taxes overall. Do I have to go thru the percentages again with a different amount to explain that? I thought not. K.I.S.S.

Before I move on to the "no deductions" part of my tax proposal, which is absolutely essential for a simple tax form and ease of calculation, I do know that at present the higher rates only apply to income which exceeds that taxed at lower rates. Marginal rates! So what? You'll also save the tax preparation fee. K.I.S.S.

To allow deductions from money transferred to you each year to reach income subject to tax for each child discriminates against childless persons. To allow deductions for home mortgage interest discriminates against persons who rent their residences. To allow deductions for charitable gifts of money discriminates against persons who volunteer only their time. And so on and so forth. Can it be that your second grade teacher didn't tell you that it is both unfair and, even worse, un-American to discriminate? No, it can't. The problem is some of you stopped paying attention in class after kindergarten. Discriminating is also time-consuming and complicated unless one engages in it at random. Third grade. And random prejudice is not discriminating at all. Consequently, there will be no lines for any deductions, or credits, except for tax payments made in advance, on the M.O.M.E.T tax return. None. Patriotism is worth some small sacrifice. And think of the pages and pages of federal tax instructions that will vanish from the earth. K.I.S.S.

Wait! Wait! Stop the presses! Individuals can deduct all other taxes paid on income for the year from gross incoming funds, including Social Security Taxes to the national government, if any. State and municipal income taxes are a mandatory division of our incoming funds between us and public corporations, not to be confused with publicly held corporations, and not actually income. Not if the correct amount is withheld from our paychecks. One line on the tax return to avoid taxes on taxes. I will leave it to wiser heads than mine to determine if the several states and their subsidiaries have to pay the M.O.M.E.T. Tax on the other taxes they collect, which are monetary transfers to them. K.I.S.S.

Is everybody ready for the very finest part of this tax proposal? The M.O.M.E.T. Tax applies whenever money changes ownership (well, almost) and sometimes when it doesn't. The recipient in each financial transaction owes an incoming funds tax on the whole amount. Pat, pat, pat your back. K.I.S.S.

Wages, salaries, and pensions are a monetary transfer to employees. Sales prices are a monetary transfer to sellers. Rents are a monetary transfer to owners. Say it with me. Service charges are a monetary transfer to providers. Stock purchases are a monetary transfer to the issuing corporation or to the previous owner of company shares. Taxed, taxed, taxed, taxed, taxed. The entire sales price of an investment is subject to the M.O.M.E.T. Tax, not solely the so-called profit or capital gain: your reward for complaining because capital gains are not indexed to inflation under current tax law. You're going to like this. Anyone who borrows money for a fixed term at a stated rate of interest owes the tax on the principal amount when they take possession of the proceeds. The purchase of bonds from the issuing corporation amounts to a loan to the company. Certificates of deposit amount to loans to the bank. K.I.S.S.

Loans will have a tax advantage because lenders are not taxed on the principal amount when the borrower transfers it back but only on the interest. It breaks my organ that pumps blood to destroy the classic clarity of the M.O.M.E.T. Tax scheme, but sales on the installment plan by the actual seller, including land contracts, are only to be taxed once as a sale and not again as a loan. Simple—the seller pays on cash or check received. To exchange money borrowed from a third party to pay for property or services from the seller is only half a stage different from a delayed cash flow sale, not a whole new creature, and so half the tax bite of a total pure M.O.M.E.T. At a real estate closing, for example, when the buyer pays the seller from mortgage proceeds, the seller will owe the estimated M.O.M.E.T. tax on the sales price and the buyer will owe the estimated M.O.M.E.T. tax on the mortgage amount. It is the lender who escapes paying the tax when the principal monthly mortgage payments are made. Since this should allow the lender to offer lower interest rates, the borrower does benefit as well. A less expensive purchase on credit when the actual seller has issued the card is taxed as one monetary transfer. Credit card purchases with the credit extended by a third party are sales/loans. *Stop this paragraph before it runs away.* Lenders must provide names of borrowers to the Internal Revenue Service upon request. Original lenders who sell promissory notes, mortgage notes, bonds, and other loan papers pay the M.O.M.E.T. Tax on the sales price. Only one untaxed payback per loan. K.I.S.S.

Me thinks that last paragraph sounds a little complicated. We are talking considerable sums of money here, not husband and wife borrowing lunch money from each other. In order to make money or monetary estimate transfer taxes practical, no M.O.M.E.T. taxes will be charged for exchanges between members of the same household.

Oh my goodness! Demand deposits in banks or other financial institutions which debit and credit sums of money to the accounts of others are not a monetary transfer to the "bank" when the money is deposited. Demand deposits are not a monetary transfer to the customer when the money is withdrawn either, provided these bank account funds are available without a penalty for "early" withdrawal and they do not earn interest for the depositor. Not taxed. I would prefer not to force everyone to pay in currency or coin for every house, car, or doctors fee for service. Checks use less paper than dollar bills. Save the trees. Funds held legally in escrow are neither taxed when deposited or disbursed. Depositing money in bank and credit accounts which don't meet the above criteria are taxed. K.I.S.S.

Gambling winnings are taxed whenever cash changes hands. Exchanges of chips during games don't count as monetary transfers. Does that make sense? I never gamble myself so I can't be sure.

Gifts that are legal tender are subject to the M.O.M.E.T. Tax unless the recipient is a relative or personal friend. Other gifts are not. Provided, the giver freely chose to make the gift and there are no conditions attached. Barter transactions are two or more separate sales. Trades of one piece of real property for another are two or more distinct sales. M.O.M.E.T. Taxes are due on the estimated sales prices so that there would have been no M.O.M.E.T. Tax disadvantage to using funny money. And so that there is still work for I.R.S. Agents. (They won't go quietly.) K.I.S.S.

I don't know what you're thinking, and I'm glad.

On to corporations and the corporate M.O.M.E.T. Tax. Did any thing about the references to sales prices in the preceding paragraphs make you uneasy? Corporations will be taxed, at lower rates, on their gross income (or the sum of the monetary transfers to them). Yes, aggregate income, not, not, *not* net. From each according to their abilities, to each according to their needs. Who said that? It distorts the capitalistic system for the more efficiently run corporations to have to pay higher income taxes than corporations with the same gross income who run up huge costs. The existing corporation formula: gross income-costs = income subject to tax. Consider company E and company I who both produced 100,000—oh, no! Not the widgets!—gidgets in a year and sold them for the same price so that each company grossed $500,000. If company E's costs for the year were $400,000, its net income was $100,000 and its income tax at 35 percent is $35,000. If company I's costs were $450,000 for a net income of $50,000, its tax at 35 percent is $17,500. Trust me, that amounts to a tax penalty of $17,500 against company E. (If Company E's lower costs endanger public safety, one could fine them instead.) Under the M.O.M.E.T. Tax, both companies would pay the same amount in "income" taxes. K.I.S.S.

Don't let it escape your notice that there will no longer be any such thing as a non-profit corporation not subject to taxes.

All financial transactions between a parent corporation and its subsidiary corporations are taxed as a monetary transfer to the recipients, if the subsid corps keep their own books and issue separate financial statements. Otherwise, no M.O.M.E.T. Tax. The corporate M.O.M.E.T. Tax should be graduated also 1 percent, 2 percent, 3 percent, etc., to reduce the tendency of American businesses to combine into one extremely inflated corporation in order to reduce the number of taxable monetary transfers. I don't mind if the bracket amount for corporations differs from the bracket amount for individuals, and if I don't, who else will? But, if I may be permitted to make one tiny suggestion, in-coming funds to sole proprietors or partnerships should be taxed at rates in between the individual and corporate rates. K.I.S.S.

After rereading the last several paragraphs, methinks I have violated the K.I.S.S. rule.

Now, isn't the M.O.M.E.T. Tax proposal keeping it simple, sirs? Once a few terms are defined? You take all your incoming funds as indicated in your bank accounts, and then settlement statements where you didn't really touch the money but it was temporarily yours for the year (for example, $75,000). Then you add any additional currency and coin payments not deposited in a bank account (say, $0) and make the adjustment for other income taxes with-held/paid or refunded—use the preceding year (for instance, $750 due after withholding, which leaves $74,250). You subtract the principal amounts of any loan repayments you received during the year (perhaps, $0, which still leaves $74,250). You subtract any monetary gifts to you from your loving spouse, not subject to this wonder tax (could be $0, which still leaves $74,250). Then you divide the bracket amount (for illustration, $10,000) into the total taxable money transfers you just got (which, in this case, would be 7.425). You round the quotient down to the nearest integer (which would, in this situation, be 7) for the tax rate that applies to you. Multiply the total taxable by the tax rate as a percent ($74,250 Times 7%) voila! Subtract the amount of M.O.M.E.T. Tax already withheld from the last calculation and you have the amount to pay, or amount due you as a refund.

And you thought it couldn't be done. You thought an easy-to-understand graduated income tax program could never be designed. One 8.5 x 11 sheet of paper to contain the instructions and the reverse side for the tax form itself. Thank you, thank you! What's that? You want me to check your answer? M.O.M.E.T. Tax=$5,197.50 for this example.

YOU SHALL NOT

You shall not kill, but need not strive
to keep the destitute alive.[1]
You shall not kill, but no offense
if you slay in self defense.
You shall not kill, but don't uphold
when the fiend has slain in cold blood.

You shall not steal, but it's okay
to overwork and underpay.
You shall not steal, but disregard
if the law permits an overcharge.
You shall not steal but push drug hooks
so the dumb become the real crooks,

Feed the hungry, if they've got money.
Heal the sick, when the fix is quick,
Build the homeless a house of cards,
but not in your back yards. And don't be a fool, forget the Golden Rule.
Do unto others as others have done unto you.

---

[1]Apology to A. Pope

VICIOUS CYCLES

Vicious cycles, sometimes referred to as vicious circles, are those situations where one damn thing leads to another curst matter which eventually leads back to the damn thing. Repeatedly. A bad example is the American tendency to build more prisons and confine people to them when the crime rate goes up. Higher numbers of prison inmates have the unfortunate effect of increasing the crime rate, which results in even more prison inmates, which further drives the crime rate in an upward direction. Welcome to the real world. Round and round we go until there is some dramatic change in social conditions.

To provide a better understanding of vicious cycles, I will discuss, what else, The Prisoner's Dilemma—a non-zero-sum game in which the two players are hypothetically arrested for a crime and separated. Each of the players has one move—either pleading "guilty" or pleading "not guilty" without knowing the move the other player makes.

There are, therefore, one, two, three, four possible outcomes of a single game. (I have found nothing written about the parameters of the game which informs me if the players are hypothetically innocent or hypothetically guilty of the crime for which they were arrested. The Prisoner's Dilemma must have been designed by a man.) The game is a trial of cooperation versus self-interest. It is my understanding the contest is scored: not guilty-not guilty=minor win-minor win; guilty-guilty=minor loss-minor loss; not guilty-guilty=major loss-major win; guilty-not guilty=major win-major loss. The results are more often expressed as the length of jail terms for the participants. The consensus of opinion is that the best winning strategy for one isolated game is to "defect" (plead guilty) rather than cooperate with the other player by making a not-guilty move.

However, when T.P.D. is played repeatedly by the same two contenders for one long match (each player being told the results of the preceding round before making a move in the next}, and a number of human persons, or computer persons, play a series of matches to determine a grand winner, the best strategy is usually the so-called "tit-for-tat" strategy. (I'll bet I can compose a longer coherent sentence than you can.) Cooperate with the other player (not the hypothetical jailers) for the first round; for the remaining rounds in the match, copy the move the other player has most recently made. For more information on Prisoner's Tournaments, see *The Evolution of Cooperation* by Robert Axelrod. I'm still working on vicious cycles.

Under the "tit-for-tat" method, if both players plead not guilty in the beginning round, wonderful. They will be cooperative for as long as the game lasts and both have wins. What they have revolving is a beneficial cycle. Yes! But if the strategy is modified to plead guilty (and attempt to defect} in the beginning round and from then on always return the other's last move, i.e., "wrong-foot-tit-for-tat," and both gamesters use it, they will forever have equal small losses. The initial guilty plea of player A brings the guilty plea of player B in the next round and then another guilty plea from A, etc. At the same time, the initial guilty plea of player B, well, I can't write about it any more. Too painful. Unless and until A and or B changes strategy they are locked in a "give me a V," "give me an I," "give me a C," "give me an I," "give me an O," "give me a U," "give me an S" cycle of non-cooperation.

What if player A uses the "tit-for-tat" scheme and player B uses "wrong-foot-tit-for-tat?" For round 1: the A move is not guilty; the B move is guilty. For round 2: the A move is guilty; the B move is not guilty. For round 3: the A move is not guilty; the B move is guilty. And so on and on, another malevolent wheel of non-cooperation for as long as the game lasts, but in this variant both players are alternating big wins with big losses unless and until A and or B changes strategy. I love games.

Let's stipulate that player A uses the "second chance tit for-tat" strategy, i.e., be nice twice, and player B uses wrong-foot-tit-for-tat? For round 1: the A move is not guilty; the B move is guilty. For round 2: the A move is not guilty; the B move is not guilty. For round 3: the A move is not guilty; the B move is not guilty. And they're off! Win-win all the way unless or until A and or B abandons tit-for-tat. Which is always possible, but not likely. Games' players are always fine, upright, and trustworthy.

It's child's play to place the theory of vicious cycles in a nutshell. Cracking them is a tad more difficult. If only I had a gavel.

WHEN MOURNING[1]

When mourning gilds the skies, my heart awakening cries,
May Jesus Christ be saved! Alike at work and prayer,
To this hope I repair, may Jesus Christ be saved!

The night becomes as day, and from the depths we say,
May Jesus Christ be saved! The powers of hatred fear,
When this sweet chant they hear, may Jesus Christ be saved!

When all the earth around, rings joyous with the sound,
May Jesus Christ be saved! If we could change the past,
Through voices true at last, Jesus Christ is saved!

---

[1]Greatly revised version of 'When Morning Gilds the Skies" by Anonymous, German. Translated
by Edward Caswell.

XMAS

What Santa Claus does one night in the year is a let's-pretend game played by most American parents, if those parents have money for gifts, with their young children. The children who've been very good get splendid presents which magically appear after Santa makes his sleigh ride; those who've been bad do not get any. Another rule is this game must be played during the birthday celebrations of our Lord and Savior, Jesus Christ.

It is regrettable that some of the children of poor parents grow up thinking they are naughty, wicked, and evil people because they never received presents from Mr. Claus at Christmas, or at least not any wonderful ones. The overly impressionable children. But we make up for it later. The bad break laws, and poor lawbreakers usually get free room and board for part of their lives at prisons built and staffed at great expense to the taxpayers.

I am so mean. I'm not going to present you with the "even the offspring of the monetarily challenged can be happy" alternative to holiday gifts from the Santa. Oh, ho! If you insist.

The 12 Days of Christmas Cookies.

Yes, on the 21st of December, Parents And Children Together mix, shape, bake, and eat fruit cake. While fruit cake is not technically a cookie, it is (usually) finger food and therefore a cookie in spirit.

And on the 22nd of December, P.A.C.T. mix, shape, bake, and eat butter star cookies in memory of the Christmas "star."

On the 23rd of December, P.A.C.T. mix, shape, bake, and eat gingerbread men, perhaps in remembrance of the human body of Christ, perhaps not.

Then on the 24th of December, traditionally Christmas Eve, P.A.C.T. mix, shape, bake, and eat sugar cookies cut out as bells. Sing while you eat, if you can.

For the 25th of December, P.A.C.T. mix, shape, bake, and eat brownies. Chocolate day. A prosaic exchange of gifts is permissible.

On the 26th of December, P.A.C.T. mix, shape, bake, and eat almond crescent cookies. The moon is also worthy of recognition.

Next on the 27th of December, P.A.C.T. mix, shape, bake, and eat date bars. I like date bars.

Then on the 28th of December, P.A.C.T. mix, shape, bake, and eat shortbread made in wedges to symbolize the Christmas tree.

On the 29th of December, P.A.C.T. mix, shape, bake, and eat coconut macaroons. By this time you're getting tired of baking cookies.

And on the 30th of December, P.A.C.T. mix, shape, bake, and eat oatmeal cookies. Make them high protein oatmeal cookies. By this time you're getting tired of eating cookies.

For the 31st of December, P.A.C.T. mix, shape, chill, and eat cheese cake. If we can make an ice cream sandwich, we can make a cheese cake cookie. The cheese will keep those of you who drink on New Year's Eve from getting drunk. I think. Ideas always need to be tested in the real world. Any volunteers?

Finally, on the 12th day of Christmas and the 1st of January, P.A.C.T. eat chocolate-dipped candies purchased from your favorite confectioner. Enjoy a baking, but not an eating, day off. I'm no fool.

You're no fool either. You will have realized the most important cookie ingredient is parents and children together. Families that bake do not forsake; they make many memories.

For children to have a Christmas vacation but not adults is ageism of the worse kind. If it's not unconstitutional it ought to be. Half days. The tough problem to solve is how to keep the cookie-eating children from turning into monsters during the holiday. I have confidence that all you parents out there will be able to hide each day's leftovers as long as necessary.

To those of you who think my repeated use of the word Christmas has changed a secular holiday into a religious one: a party in honor of the Winter Solstice by any other name is still a party in honor of the Winter Solstice.

WHY

The neatest thing I learned in Psych 101 was the theory of self-fulfilling prophecies. It means that when people think something is going to happen, they act in ways that cause that something to happen. For example, if a teacher thinks his students cannot learn, he doesn't teach properly, and woe to those students. If students think their teacher is a bad teacher, they don't try to learn, and woe to those students.

Self-fulfilling prophecies can be positive or negative. If a star basketball player chooses to join a championship team, chances are that team will continue to be an outstanding one.

As for the negative, if we think someone doesn't like us, we are apt to respond to him or her unpleasantly, and as a result, s/he doesn't like us.

If a person in pain puts off going to the doctor because s/he is afraid s/he will be told s/he is going to die, guess what? When s/he finally does go, s/he is more likely to be told s/he is going to die.

If s/he goes to bed thinking s/he won't be able to sleep, very likely the stress will keep him or her awake.

Are you getting the picture? Self-fulfilling prophecies are all around us. They explain so much. Too bad I can't think of any more at the moment. It must be writer's block.

ZODIAC

And now it's time for an astrology update. We are all, of course, familiar with the active/stable/reactive cycle that begins at the vernal equinox, at the summer solstice, at the autumnal equinox, and again at the winter solstice. You old-fashioned types night want to refer to this as the cardinal/fixed/mutable cycle. But how many of us ever think about the weather turbulence cycle triggered by sun/Mercury/earth alignments approximately every 120 days? Okay, probably somebody at the *Farmer's Almanac* does, but how about the rest of us? We also get a personal imprint after we're born. That energy/physical growth/mental growth/emotion cycle is the other major influence in our "sun" sign. It makes of us an enthusiast, a materialist, a conceptualist, or an emotionalist. It's hydrogen, oxygen, and carbon that are elements, not fire, earth, air, and water. I swear.

Very, very loosely, active personalities favor making changes; stable personalities favor maintaining the status quo; and reactive personalities accept the heavy burden of choosing between change or no change. I hope. I list:

Seasonal Personality Types (in their customary order)	Modern Image	Traditional
Active enthusiastic	Battering lamb	Aries
Stable materialistic	Contented cow	Taurus
Reactive conceptual	Inspired buffoon	Gemini
Active emotional	Starched nurse	Cancer
Stable enthusiastic	Golden jack	Leo
Reactive materialistic	Honey bee	Virgo
Active conceptual	Justice of the piece	Libra
Stable emotional	Forever moor	Scorpio
Reactive enthusiastic	Daylight gambler	Sagittarius
Active materialistic	Nanny goat	Capricorn
Stable conceptual	Calculating mule	Aquarius
Reactive emotional	Mermaid	Pisces

Simon says:

how one looks	depends in part on the time of day, and
how one reasons	depends in part on the position of the Earth
how one feels	" Moon
how one expresses thoughts	" Mercury
how one expresses emotions	" Venus
how one acts	" Mars
how one deals with prosperity	" Jupiter
how one responds to adversity	" Saturn
how one adjusts to changes	" Uranus

relative to the sun and other planets, all when one was born.

I say: the manner in which one feels depends on the phases of moon rather than on the sections of the zodiac which the moon traverses; the relevant time of day means dawn, noon, dusk, or midnight or points in between, and not the "rising sign"; and conjunctions and oppositions are the only aspects that matter.

I don't know nothing about no other aspects. But when you consider the planetary influences in your life, Mercury is male to the Sun's female, the Moon is male to the Earth's female and Saturn is male to Jupiter's female. I kid you not. But okay, Mars is male to Venus' female. Satisfied?

Here's why not. One should consider the other planetary influences when it comes to romance and marriage. Yes, indeed. One needs astronomical balance for a sound relationship was well as sexual chemistry and other good stuff. One neat pattern is the sun sign of one of you in opposition to the Venus sign of the other one of you, together with the sun sign of the party of the second part in opposition to the Mars sign of the party of the first part. Huh? (Sun one opposite Venus two; Sun two opposite Mars one.) Why is this a neat pattern? Because, in your joint birth horoscope, you have an Earth/Venus conjunction in one season of the year and an Earth/Mars conjunction in another season of the year. I'm sure there are other star maps which also work. Otherwise, finding your one true love wouldn't be nearly as much fun. Pretty please with molasses on it make sure you and your proposed significant other have a fixed design before making a commitment. This doesn't only affect you, your spouse, and any children you may have. If you marry someone who is a lousy match for you, the people you both could have married happily may not find someone else suitable either. You could inadvertently set off a chain reaction of several bad marriages or discontented singles. And people wonder why the divorce rate is so high in these United States in the latter part of the twentieth century,

What else in astrology good for? Providing insight into the character of historical figures. Legend has it Jesus of Nazareth was a Capricorn and that there was an exceptionally bright star in the sky at the time of his birth. Later astrologers speculated the star was a conjunction of planets in the spring of 7 B.C. (Or was it 6 B.C.?) Powerful but unbalanced horoscope. However, to be mythologically correct, Jesus must be an Aries, born into the same (Easter) season as the one he died from. That would mean he was conceived near the summer solstice the preceding year. Then, to become an innovator for all seasons, birth when the moon was in Libra and Capricorn was rising was called for. All active (or cardinal) signs. I presume we can be sure that the sidereal zodiac and the tropical zodiac were close together 2,000 years ago. Happy New Year!

Clues:
Eric Clapton
Judy Collins
Bob Dylan
Linda Ronstadt
Mick Jagger
Billy Preston
John Lennon
Joni Mitchell
Keith Richards
Joan Baez
Carol King
George Harrison

COLD WAR NO MORE

Listen in your mind, if you will, to a Viet Nam vet singing the entire first verse of "With God on Our Side" by Bob Dylan, (lyrics may be found in *Lyrics 1962-1985*, Bob Dylan, page 93);

Then the entire second verse;
The entire third verse;
The entire fourth verse;
And the entire fifth verse;
And the first four lines of the sixth verse;
Followed by:

But a funny thing happen'd
To all that red tide
And the Russians now too
have God on their side.

We still need armed force
It's not just our pride
You can't win a war
With just God on your side
So now we fight battles
All over this earth
How else to defend
The land of our birth?

The land of the free
And the home of the brave
Will never forget
The blessings God gave
We lost it in Nam
And we're still cursed

Without God on our side
It'd been a lot worse.

Not just for practice
The war games we play
Because a good cause
We must help in some way
When the misled Iraqis
Played into our hand
With God on our side
We drew a line in the sand.

Returning to the entire seventh verse of Dylan's lyrics;
Then the entire eighth verse;
And the first six lines of the ninth and last verse;
Followed by:

We're not on God's side
'Til we stop these damn wars!

And now you've heard the nineties version of "With God on our Side."
Well, almost.

LIGHT AND DARK

Some of us like to blame others of us for the failures of all of us. Frequently, black Americans are used as national scapegoats.

Why black goats and not goats of another color? For historical reasons? No. Because Negroes belong to an inferior race? No. No. Not since the "white" public attitude shift in the sixties. Not since the Reverend King led American descendants of slaves out of the confinement of segregation and into the wider society. But because a disproportionate number of people identified as ethnic blacks have been judged by the content of their character and found wanting.

I have no right to put down such words because I write white? Is that your position? As it happens, I am a member of a minority group that has been despised since man first walked on two legs. I am left handed!

Sinister me is convinced I would be shocked by the total number of black males incarcerated in Michigan prisons for exercising poor judgment, and no other crime, if only I knew what the number was. Expensive injustice pains me from my pocketbook straight to my heart. Regardless, we've all seen the convict statistics broken down by arbitrary racial categories. And, yeah, it is criminal to steal from other people to support a drug habit. We've all seen the unmarried teenage mother numbers by the colors also. And it is a tad irresponsible to bring children into the world in the absence of two co-parents fully prepared to care for them. Those findings demonstrate not poverty-stricken personalities but flawed dispositions to most Americans. Celebrate diversity, not perversity.

Why such a high percentage of anti-social behaviorists in the colored community? There are a zillion ways to answer that question. My personal favorite follows.

Like a tree, planted by the water, a human being has light-sensitive cells. Other things being equal, which of course they never are, the darker one's skin tone, the more skin exposure to sunshine one needs to stay healthy. Other things being equal, which of course they never are, the darker one's eye color, the more sight exposure to sunlight one needs to stay healthy. The typical urban jungle American life-style doesn't provide enough unshaded outdoor activity during the day to meet the minimum daily requirement for illumination for a minority in our society. And with lack of illumination, the vision of a beautiful future is lost.

Americans whose not-so-immediate ancestors (all of them) thrived in sub-Saharan Africa would be well advised to spend more time in bright light than their entirely Caucasian neighbors do, rather than less. Without shades. Take advice with a grain of salt; avoid sunburn. We may even hear the baaad, "You don't like me because I'm blaaack," vocals of opportunistic black kids disappear. Read on.

Together with other inexpensive therapies, such as play and no day watching of TV, light can begin healing the sick and the weary children among us. And the sun is an equal opportunity supplier.

As for those black American females who have problems because they are overly cooperative with others in their "group," their teachers could set them to playing singles' outdoor tennis matches against each other. As for those black American males who are moving toward murder or death because they are too competitive with their peers: their coaches could run them into playing softball, on grass, in teams which have the same players for an entire season. You never know. After a few years of the cure for all needy residents, baseball may once again become the number one game in these United States. Go Tigers!

ABORTION ARGUMENTS

If we permit the state to deny pregnant women safe and legal abortions, then the day will come when the state claims the right to compel women to have abortions against their will.

If we allow pregnant women to obtain safe and legal abortions, then the day will come when the state condones the active murder of living children.

Because such beings cannot speak for themselves, our first priorities must be ensuring that fetuses survive long enough to be born and that people in a non-reversible coma or vegetative state live as long as possible.

A fetus will suffer less pain from a quick death than a child will suffer from a lingering death due to starvation or diseases associated with malnourishment.

God has ordained that women obey men, and therefore the prospective father or another male authority figure should decide whether or not a pregnant woman obtains an abortion.

A child who was conceived as a result of rape cannot honor his father if he knows the circumstances of his conception and cannot honor his mother if he doesn't know the truth, and therefore pregnant rape victims should be required to obtain abortions.

Other things being equal, a woman has a better chance of surviving without her young child than that young child has of surviving without his mother, and therefore the prospective mother's right to life takes precedence.

A women's body has to be used to sustain a human fetus and a person's body should not be used for any purpose without his consent.

I

I was born in the spring of 1943. My sign is peace. One of my first words was *book*.

I am a lifelong resident of the state of Michigan, my scenic Michigan. My paternal grandfather, whose birthday was a few days prior to my own, was by occupation a dairy farmer. The only joke I remember him telling, when I asked for more milk during a meal at my grandparents' place and my mother said no, was, "It's all right, Ruth, we keep a cow." In his old age, his favorite hobby was watching the television show *To Tell the Truth*.

I am the oldest of three siblings. I have not raised any other children. My first hero was the Lone Ranger. I must say that, without the dignity of Jay Silverheels, the TV series would have been an inferior product.

I am a college graduate. I studied to become a liberal artist. For a time, I earned my living as a legal assistant. I don't know why the caged bird sings; I have some idea of why the caged panther snarls.

I am single, but not by reason of divorce. However, I did live with the same cat for eighteen years. She was part Siamese and she practically talked. I am such a romantic that, as I write this, I am contemplating matrimony with a beer-drinking alcoholic I have never met and whose name I do not know. If I ever learn to manage my case of Seasonal Affective Disorder, I will be empowered to meet him. I always have been a methodist and I always will be. The lower case "m" was intentional. Love is not all you need, You also need a code of ethics. Thank you, Archbishop of Canterbury.

My favorite color is royal blue. A paler hue won't do.

My favorite food is strawberry shortcake. I take what I eat very seriously. The berries: fresh, local produce, chilled and lightly sugared. The shortcake: a baking powder biscuit, made without sugar and warm from the oven.

My favorite black and white movie is *High Noon*. My favorite colored movie *is Star Wars-Episode IV.* I am such a conformist,

My favorite singer is Joan Baez. I will never forget the first time I heard her voice. It was in a Language lab at college. My favorite songwriter is Bob Dylan. Until I heard *Street Legal* for the second time, I didn't realize what a damn fine songwriter he was. My favorite musical group is the Rolling Stones. If you think rock music should be sung by people of all ages, you may or may not be a Stones fan, but you won't be a fan of the young sentimentalists.

My favorite author is P. G. Wodehouse. Humor is such an aphrodisiac.

My favorite philosopher is me. I am brilliant on a good day. On a bad day, I'm helpless. I have to live that way. If I were brilliant on a bad day, I would be a menace to society.

REPRODUCTION EDUCATION

Lesson I: PURPOSE
The primary mission of sexual activity is procreation.
The secondary mission of sexual activity is mutual pleasure.

Lesson 2: LINES

Seduction	Pleading
Only the good die young.	I'm so hot for you.
Only the bad seduce virgins.	Get a blow job.
You're no virgin.	I'm so cold without you.
Then I can't die young.	I'll bring you a nice, warm blanket.

Reality
If you love me, have sex with me.
    If you love me, delay and wait.
I'm off to war in the morning.
    I'll tarry until you come back.

What if I die in battle?
    If you're a man, you will return.
What if I'm not a man?
    I'll always love you,
    but I'll find a man to be the father of my children.

Lesson 3: VOWS
With God as my witness, I, *Name*, take you, *Appellation*, to be my one and only wedded wife/husband, to have and to hold from this day on, for richer and for poorer, in sickness and in health, as long as we both live. I shall always honor and cherish you and the memory of you. My home is now and hereafter your home, and I accept your kin as my own family, in law and in affection. *To the

best of my ability, I will create children we both want and not any others. I will loyally co-parent any and all of our progeny.* I give you the right to use and enjoy, according to custom and law, but not to sell or dispose of, one half of my real and personal property, and I grant you a joint interest in my future income. With this cake, I feed you; with this wine, I toast you, and with this ring, I marry you. May the Lord bless us and keep us and give us peace, together. [*...* Optional—for the young and fertile.]

ECONOMIC ETHICS

We need both free and fair enterprise. We can't have one without the other and make it last. It's bad to get paid too much just as it's bad to get paid too little. Women are being paid approximately 80 percent of what men get for non-economic reasons—because employers know they will work for less. In a conflict of interest, with negotiations, a mistake to take too much or settle for too little.

Wait a minute. How about salaries and wages based on supply and demand in the labor market? When demand for a skill in a locality goes down, perhaps everyone's paycheck who has that skill should be reduced. And likewise, when demand goes up, income should go up. Hold labor auctions every year for each type of job unless the employees have a signed contract. How many will do this job for x number of dollars? If the numbers are not met, then raise the wages or salaries paid to everyone doing the job until they are. If someone is incompetent at a certain job, they shouldn't be doing it. They are a hazard to the rest of us. This scheme above is for interchangeable labor. Persons with unique skills, like a unique physical item or house, should be sold one a time to the highest bidder. Oh, pardon me, rented for part of each day. That would be contract labor.

I fear my plan is too unsettling, even with a minimum wage law. No one would know from year to year what income they would have unless they have a commitment for extended years. Oh well, I can't think of everything. Maybe someone else can.

Why do we have personnel departments except to identify the different types of work that need to be done in the company and what skills are needed to do it?

There is some job creation even with a high unemployment rate but, for all practical purposes, with a high employment rate, if you find a job that means someone else will be out of work. When productivity per man hour of work increases and a company lays employees off instead of expanding in some way, they start a vicious cycle. Fewer people buy their product or service, so they need to lay off more people to cut costs.

No matter how much or how little people have, compulsory take-aways don't work. But it is so very divisive to have the population divided into two groups, the rich and the poor. There is very little sense of community.

For the "from each according to his ability, to each according to his need" concept to work, every worker had to have the same pay for the same hours of work. One problem with communism was the perks to party officials. The fix: keep "corrupting" power away from leaders. Another problem was workers not working because they would get paid whether they worked or not. The fix: fire them.

A new idea for job creation: pass a maximum wage law. Many people say that increasing the minimum wage decreases the number of jobs available. It would seem to follow that lowering the maximum wage would increase the number of jobs. The very opposite of supply and demand.

How about a truth in labor law? It is appropriate for U.S. to refuse to buy products made from slave labor—not interference in internal affairs of another country, I think. We should know who we are doing business with, shouldn't we? And label goods made in the U.S. of A. Or not. On the price tag for imported goods and services, state, in U.S. dollars in the week received or transferred, the average wage per hour of the lowest paid laborer involved in its production, whether paid by the hour, by the piece or on salary. We can do this now that we have computers. I would really like to see more information but I'm going easy on corporate America. If consumers want to buy goods made from low-priced labor, they should be able to? Let them make the choice.

Just a note about a self-fulfilling prophecy. Banks charging higher interest on these loans they consider riskier may cause business failures. Two businesses that had the same gross income and same costs except for interest expense might have considerable difference in net income, resulting in the failure of one. Set interest rates according to the supply of money available and don't lend the money to bad credit risks at all.

TESTING

Choose to take Drug Test A or Drug Test B. Answer yes or no to each of questions 1 and 2. Write an essay for item 3.

Test A
1. Should marijuana use be illegal because some individuals who use it later become "hard" drug addicts?
2. Should beer and wine consumption be illegal because some individuals who "drink" later become alcoholics?
3. Describe what you think would happen if the use of marijuana was no longer proscribed in the U.S.

Test B
1. Should beer and wine consumption be illegal because some individuals who "drink" later become alcoholics?
2. Should marijuana use be illegal because some individuals who use it later become "hard" drug addicts?
3. Describe what you think would happen if the use of marijuana was legalized in the U.S.

[Answers to Test A: 1. Yes, 2. Yes, 3. Subjectively scored from 10 to 0 points. Your score will be no more than 5 points if you failed to mention the end of Western Civilization as we know it.]

{Answers to Test B: 1. No, 2. No, 3. Subjectively scored from 0 to 10 points. Your score will be at least 5 points if you predicted that American cigarette companies in search of new markets would win the war for the drug consumer's dollar.}

AFFINITY

The answer is: "The American affinity for sadomasochism." So what is the question? What does the expression, "The American love affair with violence" really mean?

Fear, actual pain, and shame can be sexual turn-ons. No! But fear, pain and shame are undesirable means of arousal for spectators as well as participants. Boo! Toss me out of the horror show.

Where did said affinity come from? Virginia, some of our founding fathers who emigrated to the British American colonies seeking religious freedom had weird ideas about sexual conduct. Does the word *puritanical* ring a bell? (Others had slaves for sex.) None of that "with my body, I thee worship" rap for them. Not even if married.

Now why has that legacy not dissipated over the centuries? Packaging mayhem is a shortcut way of making big bucks. And where there is a way to make big bucks, advertising will precede it. Don't blame the movie industry exclusively; blame each and every person who pays money to watch their sex violence death combo flicks. Censure those that profit from our peculiar see-people-perish pornography. Tax those that watch lethal lust for free.

What kept sadomasochism going before the cinema arrived on these shores? We had a whole weaponry industry to whip us up. Wars and threats of war are very lucrative for people, and I use the word loosely, who own factories that manufacture munitions. Generally, all sides in a malignant conflict, foreign or domestic, buy as many guns and bombs as they can afford. Which are usually overpriced. In America in the 2000s, firing a long gun is still sexy. And seeing an explosive blow up is still a great thrill. As a nation, we have made progress. Today, seeing mangled corpses up close and personal interferes with the afterglow. So we look at our fictitious dead on a big screen instead and make out.

With what can Americans displace making war on the many? Privately making love with the one who shines the moon and brightens the stars. The raciest romance. Ah, what crimes are committed in the name of alliteration.

FIGURE OF SPEECH

Most people know Jesus of Nazareth is referred to in the King James Version of the Christian Bible as "the son of God." He is further described as "the light of the world" in the gospel according to John. Let us consider the significance of that phrase. What is literally the light of the world? The sun. Oh, gosh! A metaphor! Jesus is the sun, I wonder. Could the expression "son of God" also be a figure of speech? "Sun" and "son" are pronounced the same where I come from, so it would be particularly poetic prose if it were. Let the son shine in. *Mon deux*. I'm not satisfied yet. If one takes the English phrase "the sound of God," which could easily apply to a prophet, and translates the "s" word in it into French, *voila!* The phrase becomes "the *son* of God." Modern English "sound" and modern French "son" are not pronounced the same, but let us return to the days of Chaucer. Jesus is the sonne/sunne/soun of God. Triple play!

TIME OUT OF SYNC

It is the current, and often deplorable, practice of American politicians to give the people what they think they want because the public has been sold a false bill of goods. A prime example is the legislation which mandates resetting the official time twice a year to save daylight. I don't know how to break it to you gently, folks, but Daylight Savings Time does not save any daylight. Not one hour, not even one minute! What it actually does is screw up everybody's biological clock. This is bad! Very bad! I can't begin to tell you how bad it is. While I am pro-choice on the right of an individual to screw up his or her own biological clock, I am adamantly and unalterably opposed to messing with the biological clocks of others without their consent. Members of Congress, I call upon you to repeal all laws authorizing and requiring the so called, deceptively called Daylight Savings Time. NOW!

And while you're at it, prohibit the savage work schedules commonly known as upside-backward rotating shifts. As everyone should have learned in kindergarten, but apparently did not, if, for some unfathomable reason, rotating shifts are required, they should start with the natural first shift, time period: 4 A.M. to noon. Switch to the instinctive second shift, time period: noon to 8 P.M. Move to midnight third shift, time period: 8 P.M. To 4 A.M.

I'm ready for bed.

STATE

Michigan voters now elect members to the congressional House of Representatives with a separate geographic district for each congressperson. May I persuade you that the one person, one vote, at large system of electing congresspersons is superior? May I explain to you what I mean by the one person, one vote, one vote at large system of electing representatives? Let us assume that the state has fifteen representatives. Every voter in Michigan votes for one candidate for the whole state. The fifteen candidates with the highest number of votes are elected to Congress. It's not fair, you say. Why not? You only get to vote for one in district voting. The leaders of the political parties will have fits. The beauty of the system is the more votes the top candidates receive, the less votes others will need to be elected. Thus giving minorities a better chance that their preferences will be chosen. There are no shortcuts to good governments. We must vote in each and every election. Well, almost.

While we're at it, apply the same type of scheme to the Michigan House. Elect an odd number of Representatives, greater than the number of Senators, at large in the entire state. Each voter can vote for one candidate. The Michigan Senate elections can remain the same as they are now but with stricter rules about gerrymandering. Without gerrymandering, adopting the modest proposal suggested above may not be necessary.

The minimum age for voting in state elections should be changed to fourteen. Interest the population while they are young. Convicted felons should retain the right to vote even during their unfortunate incarcerations. No imprisonment allowed without the chance to elect the legislature that makes the laws.

Speaking, I mean writing, of crime, the state police should enforce state laws and local police should enforce local laws. Of course cooperation will be needed. When juries were originally established, the community probably would know who did the killing/committed the crime. What had to be deliberated was the question of justifiable homicide or murder/willful injury or accidental injury. Also, was there any reason for theft? That's why a jury of the accused's peers was chosen. The Michigan legal system perhaps should be changed so that the police have the responsibility to discover who did the deed, with a judge or grand jury to decide if they have proved their case and then another jury to decide if the action should be considered a crime. And another jury to appeal to if the facts are in dispute. Too many juries when it's difficult to find enough people to sit on juries now? Perhaps. I can't solve every problem. There would be a dilemma if an innocent person had to plead the action he did not commit wasn't criminal. But the same problem exists now in the penalty phase of a trial.

Finally, because the state police would have more responsibility, there should be state as well as local property taxes and differing property tax rates for land with and without structures. How about so much per acre for unoccupied land? There will not be many municipal services needed by the owners. Tax buildings at so much per square foot. I could go on, but I won't.

HIT OR MISS

Who and what made Adolf Hitler of Austria and Germany the monstrous man he was?

Try this for size: When he was a young man, someone comprehensively convinced Herr Hitler that his mother was responsible for his troubling neuroses. Someone in Vienna who was practicing psychiatry without a license during the years Hitler lived there. Yes, I do mean Dr. Freud.

In actual fact, it had been his father who brutally abused him and his beloved mother. And after his final treatment, for the rest of his life, his psychic torment was immense because his mind was divided against itself. He sought revenge for his suffering.

ENDS VS. MEANS

The end justifies the means is an invalid English sentence. Why is that common expression invalid? Because the means applied decide the end obtained. Ends can't vindicate anything. They are results determined by what goes before.

As an example, people can't use lethal force to obtain peaceful objectives. Sooner or later, more lethal force will occur. People retaliate. One can only successfully use lethal force when one's objective is death and destruction.

Two of the most successful military operations in U.S. history were the Berlin airlift and the Cuban missile blockade. Neither required a shot being fired.

What about World War II, you ask? Didn't the Allies use death and destruction to pacify Europe? Well the Germans started it and they lost, didn't they? And who's to say it wouldn't have ended sooner and with less loss of life if the Allies had used non-violent tactics to "win." Then there was the Marshall Plan. Without it WWII may have led to World War III.

RESURRECTION RUMOR

First thing first. Rape or seduction, the biological father of Jesus of Nazareth is more likely to have been a Roman than a Jew or a god. I see him as a civil engineer, not a military fighter. Not one shred of historical evidence for that idea though.

Why not the God as a father? It is immoral to get a virtuous young woman with child if one is unable to marry her because of some impediment. Mary was a virtuous young woman. God is a "moral" supreme being, and a moral supreme being would not commit an immoral act. *Ergo* God did not "get" Mary with child.

Is the murder of one person by other persons ever cause for celebration? How's that for an engaging philosophical question?

Does it depend on the murder? Would a judicial murder, an unjust killing disguised as a lawful execution, be an acceptable excuse for a festive feast if we liked the judge and had disliked, or even hated, the condemned? Okay, we're only human; maybe. But how about vice versa? How does the idea of a judicial murder when we disliked the magistrate and liked, or even loved, the victim strike you? As party time? No. I write for almost everyone when I write no.

Why then do we make an exception in the case of the Emperor of Rome versus Jesus of Nazareth, Pilate presiding?

I can hear you all yelling, or screaming, that it is the resurrection that Christians celebrate each Easter, not a death by torture. Well, almost. Can you hear me shouting back, "No murder, no resurrection"? I tell you, there would have been no spectacular return to the land of the living if Jesus had died of old age or other unassisted natural causes. I do not compel you to believe me, but if you agree, and you wish to think logically, you must also agree that, therefore, one's happiness at Easter depends on that particular crucifixion having occurred twenty centuries ago.

The crucifixion was as bad a tree as there ever was. Can a bad tree give good fruit? You may decide. I am stuck between a house built on a stone foundation and a ship beached on the sand.

However, I suspect that a bad tree always produces rotten fruit. I further suspect that the alleged physical resurrection of Jesus Christ is the greatest rumor ever spread.

So why have so many for so long believed in this triumphant hearsay? Because the disciples of Jesus devoutly accepted the Easter narrative as true. The remaining eleven personally chosen followers believed l) because they simply wanted to; 2) because the man-god suffering to save his people makes such a resplendent yarn; and 3) because the earthly remains of Jesus disappeared within three days after entombment.

When calmness returns, one can divide rumors into three categories—those that are false, those that are true, and those that are partly false and partly true. If the resurrection rumor is false, or partly false, the question that really needs to be answered is, "What happened to the dead body?" The manipulative Judas Iscariot stole it and disposed of it, by fire or by sea.

MENTAL ILLNESS

If you (singular) have an excess of serotonin and a scarcity of melatonin in your brain, I conclude you will be manic. Hee! Try bright light in the morning and complete darkness at night.

If you (singular) have a scarcity of serotonin and an excess of melatonin in your brain, I suppose you will be drowsy depressive. Hi! Anyone for warm milk and honey?

If you (singular) have a scarcity of serotonin and a scarcity of melatonin in your brain, I deduce you will be insomniac depressive. Ho! Take a guess.

If you (singular) have an excess of serotonin and an excess of melatonin in your brain, I suspect you will be suicidal. Hum! Seek help quickly.

Hope I got them right.

Use home remedies with extreme caution and for mild cases only.

Serotonin and dopamine are antagonistic; they don't coexist well. If you (singular) have too little dopamine in your brain during the day and too much at night, you will be schizophrenic. Who!

The fight-or-flight response of adrenaline is really a fight, flight, or freeze response. If you (singular) are a schizophrenic under stress and a man, you are more apt to be paranoid or hyperactive. Fear responses. If you (singular) are a female schizophrenic under stress, you are more apt to be paranoid catatonic. If you missed doing some very important work when ill and are afraid you will do it again, you get subacute and chronic catatonic schizophrenia. You suffer from a delusion that you are physically exhausted. That condition is better known as chronic fatigue syndrome. Whoa!

In the beginning, complete bed rest being debilitating, you may eventually become physically incapable of exertion. With hyperactivity, in the beginning, you suffer from a delusion that you cannot sit still and concentrate on one subject for more than a brief period of time. In the end, you do become incapable of it. With anorexia, in the beginning, you suffer from a delusion that you are fat. In the end, your body will no longer tolerate food. With obesity, in the beginning, you suffer from a delusion that you are starving. In the end, you must eat constantly or you will starve.

Estrogen causes more sensitivity to light and testosterone makes you responsive to heat. Enough said? Ha!

The foregoing -ins, -ens, -ines, and -ones are either hormones or neurotransmitters which are manufactured within from nutrients absorbed. To maintain their brain's normal chemical balance, human beings, generally, need to consume fewer foods containing the amino acid tryptophan and fewer high carbohydrates foods with more exposure to light. That is to say, warm milk and cookies are a remedy for what ails us only in the fall. The tryptophan and carbohydrates combination is needed to produce serotonin; darkness and cholesterol are needed to produce melatonin. If you haven't memorized the list of cholesterol containing foods, there's not much hope for you. Eat extra proteins to reduce serotonin levels and/or increase dopamine; "see" more strong light to lower melatonin levels. Okay?

"If anything can go wrong, it will" applies to biochemical systems as well as mechanical ones, and one's mind and body are one biochemical system—a hyperactive chem lab with a life span. We are what we eat and what we think and what we perceive and what we do held together by skin and bones. Well, almost. It is impossible to distinguish between a mental illness and a physical illness in a human being, and I am not one to attempt the impossible.

People catch the above disorders the same way they catch a cold, through a combination of psychological stresses, poor (for them) diet, physical stresses, and a virus. I wouldn't like to guarantee we can't catch them from bacterial infections either. What part of us takes the biggest hit depends. On what? I don't know. There, I've said it. I've confessed I don't know everything.

Sometimes people do recover from a disordered biochemistry that noticeably affected their mental processing without active intervention. Sometimes their brain starts chasing its tail (I know it's a lousy metaphor) and won't stop without being physically halted for a time. And sometimes, miserable us, the condition becomes more or less chronic.

If the last disease alternative has overtaken you, or to someone you love, you might like to know that the fictitious Dr. Frasier Crane, the fictitious Dr. Niles Crane, and the fictitious Dr. Lilith Sternum are the only three psychiatrists left in the entire United States that have never heard of neurotransmitters and their receptors. Well, almost. And the real psychiatrists are permitted by law to write prescriptions for medications that have far fewer side effects than a bottle of booze.

I must be honest. There is a chronic illness that can't be successfully treated with "pills": Post Traumatic Stress Syndrome. The only way for you

P.T.S.S. people to recover from being witness to or victim of a natural catastrophe, or a major accident, or human terrorist acts is to describe the details of the experience to someone. Don't try this at home, kids. There are therapists who can help out there somewhere.

However, if you have Repressed Post Traumatic Stress Syndrome, you have convinced yourself that your nightmarish, horrible, and unreal incident(s) was/were only bad dream(s); it or they never actually happened. There are three serious difficulties with this practice: 1) felonies may go unreported, 2) every time you go to sleep you have to re-convince yourself your memories are dreams, and 3) you develop a very unpleasant personality. What you need is a good psychoanalyst, but you don't know it. And even if you did know it, I'm not sure there are any available. What does it matter? If this paragraph applies to you, by tomorrow you will have forgotten that you read it.

To be artistically creative and mentally ill means sports analogy coming up. The mind-impaired virtuoso's situation is like that of the physically injured Kirk Gibson limping up to the plate for the L.A. Dodgers in the last half of the ninth inning of the first game of the 1988 World Series. On that night, Gibson was not fit to run the bases. So, if he wanted to score a run, and Gibson did, he had to hit a home run. (Dodgers won the game and the series against the Oakland Athletics. Does anyone remember if KG helped?)

ASS

Perhaps this chapter should be entitled "MULE," but I have too many "A"s and not enough "M"s in my scheme. Islands can be blockaded. Even large islands. Expensive and time consuming but doable.

NIGHTMARE

I have no evidence for my unorthodox Watergate conspiracy theory. Let me make that perfectly clear: I have no evidence. Mr. Nixon's character is not evidence.

Some famous general said sometime somewhere, "A retreat is the most difficult of all military maneuvers to execute successfully," or words to that effect. When Richard M. Nixon became President of the United States, the U.S. of A. was fighting an undeclared war in Southeast Asia. I suppose (based on his public statements) that President Nixon thought, from a national security viewpoint, it would be dangerous to give up the American cause and unilaterally withdraw U.S. military forces from Viet Nam. Other sovereign nations might think we were weak, vacillating, and unwilling to fight to protect our interests. At the same time, what the Viet Cong were doing to American forces in South Viet Nam was something similar to what the colonists had done to the British troops during the battle of Lexington and Concord during our Revolutionary War. We all know who won that battle, don't we? What Mr. Nixon needed to get our soldiers out of Viet Nam was a very careful plan of retreat.

Furthermore, the retreat had to be carried out in the face of those American voters who emphatically did not want American troops withdrawn until the Viet Nam war was won by the "right" side.

You way think it would have been impossible to design and perform such a strategic scheme. But your name is not, I presume, Mr. Richard "Machiavelli" Nixon. The sensational piece-by-piece unveiling of the White House cover up of the Watergate burglary distracted the attention of the American people from the fighting, from the body count, from the Viet Cong advances. During Mr. Nixon's second term, the suspicion that a sitting President had committed impeachable offenses was the foremost story, the most important story, on the national television newscasts and in the daily newspapers for a considerable length of time. The war wasn't totally forgotten, but its impact back home was diminished. As for foreign nations, their leaders could have been told that, were it not for the petty domestic political affair called Watergate taking up so much of President Nixon's time, the eventual outcome would have been peace in Viet Nam on American terms. I caution you, *could have* been doesn't mean they were. Ask someone at the State Department what the administration line was. I can't. I'm very shy about conversing with strangers.

Did President Nixon consciously sacrifice his presidency and his good name, such as it was, in an attempt to extricate the United States from a disastrous venture abroad? It is my understanding that he had the necessary skills to be able do it. I can almost see Nixon in his presidential office painstaking selecting 18.5 minutes of non-incriminating conversation on a tape and then erasing it to create the suspect gap. I can almost hear him surreptitiously feeding the "Deep Throat" info that he wanted to surface next in *The Washington Post* to the intermediary to their hotshot reporters. I do not forget that by the time Mr. Nixon resigned as President, the Honorable Gerald Ford had been elected his successor by the Congress and Mr. Secretary Kissinger was safely ensconced in an outside the White House government office. And then I wake up and tell myself that no man ever born would lead patriotic soldiers on such a torturous way home. And I leave the question at the beginning of this paragraph unanswered.

I intend to answer another question instead. Where did the sad saga of serious U.S. involvement in Viet Nam begin? It began with Joseph P. Kennedy Sr. It was noticeable that all of Mr. Kennedy Sr.'s sons died young, save one. The stylish widow of one actually married a Greek with tragedy in his own family. That one son who did reach old age accidentally killed someone young. Not a happy family.

If Mr. Kennedy Sr. had not wanted one of his sons to be elected President of the United States, no matter what the cost, John F. Kennedy would not have selected Lyndon B. Johnson to be his running mate in 1960. If Senator Kennedy had not selected Senator Johnson as his running mate, Lyndon Johnson would not have been elected Vice-President when John Kennedy was elected President of the United States. If Johnson had not have been elected Vice-President when Kennedy was elected President, good old boys in Texas (an anti-union state during the American North/South conflict in the 1860s) would not have sat around in their bars contemplating aloud how fortunate it would be if something happened to President Kennedy so Vice-President Johnson could replace him in office and show those commies a thing or two. I have a terrific imagination. If good old boys in Texas had not been discussing, while drinking, the stirring possibilities of President Johnson, the person or persons who assassinated President John F. Kennedy in Dallas would not have been roused to act with such deadly violence. He or they would have done something else with his or their hostilities. Start reading your local daily newspaper if you are skeptical of the preceding statement.

If President Kennedy had not been killed with malice, Lyndon Johnson would not have succeeded to the presidency upon his death. Stay with me. If Mr. Johnson, a man who was accustomed to use strong arm tactics to gain his objectives, had not become President, and at a time in American history when the military industrial complex was in a growth mode [source: President Eisenhower], there would have been no Gulf of Tonkin resolution. Now I admit I stretched my line of reasoning taut with that last assertion. But not so tight it broke. If the U.S. Congress had not passed the Gulf of Tonkin resolution, we, as a foreign army, navy, and air force, would not have heavily intervened in Viet Nam's primitive war in the 1960s. We had civil rights issues of our own to settle. And that's the truth.

I supposed a few paragraphs ago that President Nixon thought the U.S. would be threatened in the future by simply reversing the direction of our troop movement in 1973. I also suppose that that man went to his grave thinking, if he had won of the 1960 presidential election instead of Kennedy, then no Vietnamese nightmare for his native country. Only for them. I tend to agree. What I wonder is whether an alternative sequence of events (begun by Mr. Nixon's election as president in 1960) would have been better or not better for the nation and the world? What am I writing? Any good con man's scenario omits any and all acts of violence.

For future reference, when given the choice between electing the son of the son of a gun or the son of a Quaker for President of the United States, vote for the son of a Quaker. But even better would be electing a female offspring of a member of the Society of Friends as President of us all. Mothers, don't let your daughters grow up without any political ambitions. When a female becomes the President, of the United States of America, the occupant can no longer be described as the most powerful man in the world. Don't you know that phrase goes to male heads? They have quite a problem with keeping their testosterone levels steady, the poor guys.

I myself grew up with no personal political ambitions. My mother wanted to be a teacher when she was young; I had a dream of becoming a librarian. Writing has always been such a difficult task for me; it was many years before I realized, with that kind of background, it was inevitable that I author a strictly educational book. Are you laughing, or does your head ache? Take two aspirin and go to bed. You'll feel better in the morning, if not sooner. Over and out!